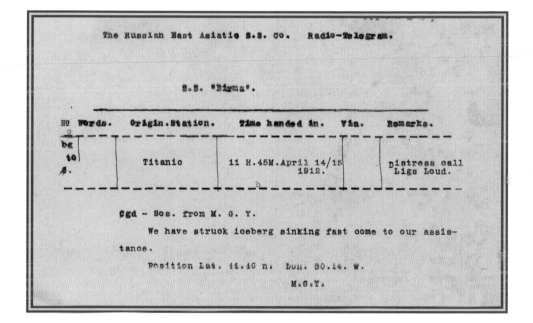

The Russian East Asiatic S.S. Co.   Radio-Telegram.

S.S. "Birma".

№ Words.	Origin.Station.	Time handed in.	Via.	Remarks.
bg to ß.	Titanic	11 H.45M.April 14/15 1912.		Distress call Ligs Loud.

Cgd - Sos. from M. G. Y.

    We have struck iceberg sinking fast come to our assis-
tance.

    Position Lat. 11.46 n. Lon. 50.14. w.

        M.G.Y.

GREAT SHIP DISASTERS

KIT AND CAROLYN BONNER

MBI

LOOKING FRD.

This edition first published in 2003 by MBI Publishing Company, Galtier Plaza, Suite 200, 380 Jackson Street, St. Paul, MN 55101-3885 USA

MBI Publishing Company titles are also available at discounts in bulk quantity for industrial or sales-promotional use. For details write to Special Sales Manager at Motorbooks International Wholesalers & Distributors, Galtier Plaza, Suite 200, 380 Jackson Street, St. Paul, MN 55101-3885 USA

ISBN: 0-7603-1336-9

On the front cover: The burning SS *L'Atlantique* drifts in the English channel. That smoke was so thick it was impossible to launch boats on the portside, and the starboard side was difficult at best. The death toll was 19, and if the ship had carried a full complement of passengers, the death poll would have been in the hundreds. *TIM*

On the frontispiece: A copy of a wireless to the East Asiatic Steamship Company vessel SS *Birma* from the HMS *Titanic*. *Author's collection.*

On the title page: This was a damage to the *Olympic* from the collision with the *Hawke* on September 20, 1911. The *Olympic* was holed in two 80 feet from the stern. Although the damage was not mortal to either ship, it required a return to a dockyard for repair in both cases. Note the two workmen in the bottom right of the image. *Courtesy Ulster Folk and Transport Museum*

On the back cover: A U.S. Coast Guard high endurance cutter. the USCG cutter *Herndon*, has a massive collision hole abaft of its bridge on the port side. The flagship of Coast Guard Division 3 was hit while on patrol by the steamship SS *Lemuel Burrows* on January 15, 1932, in dense fog off Montauk Point, Conneticut. To compound matters, the *Burrows* attempted to tow the *Herndon*, but the line snapped and the hapless cutter disappeared into the peasoup fog. Another U.S. Coast Guard vessel, the Revenue Cutter *Acushnet* came to the *Herndon's* rescue and towed it to Boston for repairs. *Author's collection*

Edited by Amy Glaser
Designed by Brenda Canales

Printed in China

CONTENTS

PREFACE

The sea awaits the innocent, and it stalks the arrogant, careless, foolish, and those who taunt its power. A wave may look beautiful crashing into a cliff, but it contains thousands of pounds of fast-moving water that is quite capable of killing a human being.

In itself, the sea can be a deadly menace. Add, however, the elements of fire, collision, explosion, crime, terrorism, and the simple unknown at sea, and what is created is an even more deadly adversary for man. There are certain truths inherent in sea travel that man tends to ignore. One of them is that you can never be too prepared. Even with maximum preparation, an accident can occur in a fraction of a second.

Great Ship Disasters chronicles recent tragedies that befell ships worldwide at port and sea. The ships featured range from the most celebrated (the RMS *Titanic* in 1912) to the unheard of outside professional maritime circles, such as the tanker *Jessica* and the M/V *Dona Paz*.

The loss of human lives from the *Titanic* was 1,512, whereas the M/V *Dona Paz* claimed 4,341 lives when she collided with the inter-island gasoline-loaded tanker M/V *Vector*. The *Titanic* holds a place in our hearts and minds that rivals other twentieth-century tragedies such as the suicide of Marilyn Monroe, the death of Princess Diana, and the assassination of John F. Kennedy. The human loss aboard the *Dona Paz*, however, was nearly three times that of the *Titanic*, yet it barely rated more than a few days worth of attention in 1987. *Great Ship Disasters* explores the rationale behind this disparity.

The interest in the *Titanic* never seems to end, and now the very same vessels (the Russian *Akademik Keldysh* and its submersibles *MIR 1* and *MIR 2*) that provided James Cameron his first views of the *Titanic* for his 1997 blockbuster film have been employed to seek out and film the former German battleship *Bismarck* and its adversary, the Royal Navy's HMS *Hood*. Locating and filming shipwrecks has become an international business. The same three-vessel team assisted with the undersea location of the Russian guided missile submarine SSGN *Kursk (K-141)*.

This book is dedicated to the thousands of men and women who face danger every day aboard ships of all types to transport people and products, as well as the men and women of coast guards and naval services in all nations. The unwritten law of the sea is that a call for help will be answered despite the peril, and these people respond whether on land or sea. When a dock fire occurs, the local fire departments come to the rescue, and like the New York Fire Department on September 11, 2001, they may not know what they will face. Yet, this does not prevent them from responding and doing their job. This book is further dedicated to those who have lost their life or who have been injured in a disaster at sea.

For Carter, Susan, and For-Shing. Without them, I would not be here today. I will be forever grateful for their care and thoughtfulness.

—Kit Bonner

INTRODUCTION

The nineteenth and twentieth centuries witnessed the greatest number of migrations in history, and, by in large, these people traveled by sea. One of the most prominent migratory paths was from Europe to the United States, with the majority of ships available unofficially deemed "cattle boats." This title comes from the time when cattle were carried from the stockyards of the New World to the hungry people of the Old World. The filth was hosed out of ship holds, temporary wooden privies were installed, and poor immigrants who wanted to come to the United States paid anywhere from $10 to $50 for the miserable trip that

The early twentieth century saw sea travel set sail like never before. Families wanted to emigrate to a new world of untold riches, where, at the least, a better life awaited them. For less than $50, a person could travel in steerage on the finest ships, such as the RMS *Olympic* (left) or the RMS *Titanic* (right), from Great Britain to the Port of New York. RMS stood for Royal Mail Service and meant that the ship carried mail and had the accompanying (and lucrative) national mail contracts. *Courtesy Ulster Folk and Transport Museum*

Today, not many people travel by ship as a mode of transportation. Yet, pleasure cruises are the modern way of sailing the seas. This vessel, one of four *Princess*-class vessels, displaces 77,000 tons and is 856 feet long. A person can enjoy a luxurious cruise in the Caribbean for just over $2,000. These ships carry nearly 1,000 crew and hotel service staff for the more than 2,500 passengers when fully loaded. The vessels are powered by economical diesel powerplants and offer far more than what was offered as first class aboard the RMS *Titanic*. Unfortunately, despite technological advancements, the ships are still subject to the same dangers at sea as their predecessors. Of course, they still can sink! *Courtesy Princess Lines*

The former SS *Independence* moored at perhaps her final berth, the Suisun Bay Reserve Fleet at Benecia, California, in July 2002. The *Independence* and her sister ship, the SS *Constitution,* were built just after World War II. The *Independence* entered service in February 1951 and had a Mediterranean route from New York to Cannes, Genoa, Naples, and back to New York. The *Constitution* followed virtually the same route and was momentarily famous for its role in the film *An Affair to Remember,* which starred Cary Grant and Deborah Kerr. Later, the *Constitution* carried Grace Kelly to Monaco amid great fanfare, for her wedding to Prince Rainer in 1956. Both vessels were originally built for the American Export Lines and displaced 23,719 tons. They were 683 feet long with a beam of 89 feet and a top speed of 26.15 knots. Both vessels could carry 1,000 passengers total in first class, cabin class, and tourist. Due to the possible need for ships in time of war, they were able to be quickly converted to troop ships and embark with up to 5,000 passengers onboard. The ships were never used in this role.
The *Constitution* was also part of the American Classic Lines, which operated in the Hawaiian Islands. The *Constitution* was lost under tow on its way to Portland, Oregon, to be scrapped in 2000. *Author's collection*

might have taken three weeks or more. The immigrant trade or steerage/third-class passenger was born, and the destinations increased to Australia, Canada, South Africa, and New Zealand. The immigration trade became very lucrative, and as demand grew for space aboard anything that would float, better ships with improved arrangements for its occupants were built.

This increased demand meant, of course, that more shipping lines in Germany, Britain, France, and the United States competed within this new trade. From all of this, the great liners of the early twentieth centu-

ry (RMS *Olympic* and SS *America*) grew. As point-to-point passage gave way to ocean cruising, an entire new form of ship travel emerged—the luxury cruise industry. That is a story of its own, and this industry includes such shipping lines as Carnival Cruiselines, Cunard, Princess, and Pacific & Orient. It also includes a bevy of companies that seems to come and go each season, dependent on the whims of their ships and creditors. Usually, the companies die when a ship sinks or the number of passengers carried falls below a minimal level in a season. Creditors take hold and seize whatev-

The bulk carrier, or "bulker," SS *Star Ismene,* is a relatively new vessel. It has its own onboard crane system, modern lifeboat launch system, and its circular accommodation ladders aft are the latest technology. It is shown here loading cargo in the small inland Port of Sacramento, California. There are thousands of bulk carriers that roam the seas, aside from the container ships that replaced the old tramp steamers. They carry a crew of 40 to 50, and over the last quarter century, more than 300 bulk carriers have sunk, with a death toll of 1,000 crew members. *Author's collection*

The savior of ships: a private salvage vessel. The *Salvage Chief* is based out of Astoria, Oregon. This powerful ship, designed to pull vessels out of trouble, has saved many a ship, as has her predecessors. Like the U.S. Coast Guard, the crew that mans the *Salvage Chief* goes out in almost any weather to save ships and lives. The *Salvage Chief* works for profit and takes a percentage of what is salvaged—a tradition almost as old as sailing ships. Crew members are salvage experts, and they know what can and cannot be done to save a vessel. One crew was certain that it could save the bulk carrier M/V *New Carissa*, stranded north of Coos Bay, Oregon, in 2000, but bureaucratic delays allowed wind and wave to push the grounded ship out of the reach of the *Salvage Chief. Author's collection*

er assets these shipping lines have. It is normally one or two elderly passenger vessels with excellent pedigrees, but they are far beyond their useful life span. These old ships find their way to the backwaters of a harbor or a scrap yard. Occasionally, fires mysteriously break out on these vessels and they are lost, only to be mourned by insurance companies and harbor officials who want to remove these menaces.

It is the ships lost at sea during a storm, with distress rockets and frantic radio signals sent out to anyone who will listen, that are the focus of adventure novels, magazines, and films. While such disasters at sea do occur, of course, we rarely get a glimpse of them in progress. The movie *The Perfect Storm* is an example of this phenomenon. No one truly knows what happened aboard the sword boat *Andrea Gail*, for there were no survivors and few radio transmissions.

Most ship disasters are dramatic, split-second events. Many occur at night and recollections are poor. News accounts are sketchy and sometimes even embellished to sensationalize. By in large, the greatest loss of human life has been aboard poorly operated inter-island ferry systems worldwide, from the South China Sea to the Baltic. The M/V *Estonia* was lost in

The iron bones of the sailing vessel *Peter Iredale,* which ran aground on treacherous sandbars near the entrance to the Columbia River in Oregon on October 6, 1906. Today, it is the most photographed shipwreck on the Pacific Coast. It was once a beautiful four-mast bark, and the owners received a paltry $500 for their claim. *Author's collection*

1984 with 852 deaths, most of whom never made it out of their sleeping quarters. There have been continuous losses of inter-island ferries in the Greek Islands and South China Sea.

In December 1987, the single greatest maritime disaster in the history of the sea happened when the Sulpicio Lines super-ferry M/V *Dona Paz* collided with the small gasoline tanker M/V *Vector.* The death toll was 4,341. Since the late 1980s, 9,526 innocent men, women, and children have perished on what were supposed to be safe and short cruises. Poorly trained staff, rotten fire hoses, inadequate life preservers, insufficient life rafts and lifeboats, and broken-down radio and radar equipment made many of these ferry boats less safe than the RMS *Titanic.* There has also been evidence of crew and officer complacency and graft, corruption, and drunkenness among those who are responsible for the safety of passengers. Often, passengers were admitted at the last moment if they paid the crew extra money, which resulted in the

severe overloading of these vessels. While ships like the *Dona Paz* are rated to hold less than 2,000 passengers, they often carry up to three times that number. The motivation is profit. An additional hazard is cargo stowage, which is not always up to safety standards. In any type of heavy weather, cargo can be expected to shift and make the vessel more difficult, if not impossible, to manuever, and inadequate stowage can add to the risk of disaster.

Unfortunately, governments, shipping line owners, and others associated with these disasters are reluctant to talk about these wrecks and losses. As an example, the local coast guard of the Philippines is under the control of the department of transportation and is organized into 60 stations. The craft include newer vessels of the *Bay* class that can accommodate up to 300 survivors and can reach 24 knots. These boats can also carry a search and rescue helicopter. However, these vessels are the cream of the crop, and most of the coast guard operations/naval forces of most

The former destroyer USS *Towers* (DDG-9) slides under the surface of a very calm Pacific after being employed as a target vessel in mid-October 2002. The 40-year-old destroyer was struck by an anti-ship missile by the frigate USS *Sides* (FFG-14). The sinking was quiet except for the sound of air escaping from within the ship as water filled interior compartments. There are few photographic images of ships foundering, and virtually none that resembled that of the RMS *Titanic*. *U.S. Navy*

Third-World nations are out of date, and many of the vessels are hand-me-downs from wealthier nations. Much of the Philippine Coast Guard relies upon its 4,000-member reserve force and large-engine-powered-outrigger-canoe-type "banca" boats for assistance with emergencies, which can take place on the vast seas that surround that nation's 7,000 islands.

Despite the fact that passenger cruise service has been eclipsed by the airliner, not all areas of the world have airfields, and not everyone can afford airfare. Personal travel by sea will remain a travel option for years to come.

Bulk cargo also travels by sea. Even with the pro-liferation of oil and gas pipelines, bulk oil is still transferred by sea, as is most bulk cargo. The number of small cargo ships has declined, but the number of container ships that ply the world's seas has increased. The automobile business would come to a grinding halt without car-carrying sea vessels from Japan or the transporters of auto and truck parts that navigate the Mississippi River and other waterways. In October 2002, a 10-day strike by longshoremen against the Pacific Maritime Association stacked up more than 60 ships along the western coast of the United States and paralyzed trade. Some companies attempted to employ freight-carrying aircraft, but their expense and limited capacity made matters worse. In spite of man's technological and transportation advances, the sea still covers 75 percent of the globe and must be utilized to meet the world's needs.

Inside, *Great Ship Disasters* showcases the past 100 years at sea. You'll embark on a powerful journey that continues to this day and encounter the difficulties that the men and women who sail the seas face. You'll experience tales of survival and lost hope. Finally, you'll uncover modern-day efforts to ensure a safer existence for those who spend their lives at sea.

CHAPTER 1

A U.S. Coast Guard high-endurance cutter, the *Herndon,* displays a massive collision hole abaft its bridge on the port side. The flagship of Coast Guard Division 3 was hit January 15, 1932, by the steamship SS *Lemuel Burrows* while on patrol in dense fog off Montauk Point, New York. To compound matters, the *Lemuel Burrows* attempted to tow the *Herndon,* but the line snapped and the hapless cutter disappeared into the pea-soup fog. Another U.S. Coast Guard vessel, the revenue cutter *Acushnet,* came to the *Herndon*'s rescue and towed it to Boston for repairs. *Author's collection*

PASSENGER, CARGO, CRUISE SHIP, AND OTHER VESSEL DISASTERS

In general, maritime disasters are the result of three major factors:

Elements of the sea. Although man sometimes contributes to the impact of these situations, the sea and its natural elements are the primary culprits. This includes storms, fog, high seas, swells, winds, icebergs, shifts in underwater terrain, such as sandbars, and other dangers to navigation.

Man-made or assisted. This category includes mutiny, poor food preparation, and inadequate sanitation. It can also include disregard for the power of the sea or bravado that can endanger the lives of crew and passengers.

Unexplained and mysterious. Piracy, barratry, terrorism, hijacking, and numerous other occurrences fall into this category. They are "unexplained" losses because these acts can cause an accident at sea so catastrophic that no S O S can be sent, thus there is little or no evidence of the cause of the loss.

Elements of the Sea

Waves, wind, shifting currents, rain, sleet, fog, and ice, sink and damage countless vessels and will continue to do so as long as men and women sail. However, many sea disasters can be prevented. Most don't just "happen." The men and women aboard the ships or dockside somehow contribute to the events, perhaps by causing a single accident that begins a chain reaction of events that leads to catastrophe. However, man plays a lesser role than nature. A tidal wave that strikes a quiet anchorage is considered an act of God, though if a boat is properly moored by an experienced seaman, chances of survival are greater than if the vessel is tied down by an amateur. This is an example where the interaction of the sea and related elements comes into play with man. Ship disasters that only involve the sea or related elements are less prevalent today.

Ships founder, capsize, or collide with one another every day. Swamping or running into mines or other dangerous floating objects that can punch a hole in the side of a vessel are less common. This still happens, though, and may explain the mysterious loss of a ship.

Between the U.S. Coast Guard, other nation's coast guards or coastal patrols, mariner societies, and other organizations, technological advances have diminished the effects of the sea on ships. Loran-C, fathometers, radar, improved radar, and weather tracking systems have been put in place to let mariner's know what weather is ahead, behind, and around them. This helps determine the sea state their vessel will encounter. The International Ice Patrol was established as a result of the RMS *Titanic* disaster to warn ships of icebergs and dangerous iceflows in the Atlantic. Firefighting schools are operated by the U.S. Navy, U.S. Coast Guard, and private companies on the Gulf Coast and in California.

In addition to fire, ice, and other maladies that plague shipping, there always seems to be fog. Fog is beautiful to those ashore but frightening to those afloat. Fog, the mariner's curse, accounts for many accidents, despite the abundance of sophisticated radar. A radar screen on an old merchant ship in a crowded harbor in the midst of thick fog has as much clutter on the screen as there is blank whiteness outside the bridge hatchway. Foghorns, bells, and whistles are signals that further confuse mariners. Many vessels collide in foggy conditions or in crowded harbors.

Another common malady is the simple fact that ships age and many are not properly cared

The White Star Line steamship SS *Republic*. The *Republic* was considered second-rate to a degree, because it catered mainly to the North American immigrant trade and was considered more of a North Atlantic ferry boat. She displaced 15,378 tons when christened in 1903 and was 585 feet in length. The *Republic* carried up to 200 first-class passengers and 2,000 steerage-class travelers. She became famous on January 23, 1909, when she was involved in a major collision with the SS *Florida* near the *Nantucket* lightship. The collision was fatal and all but four of her passengers and crew were saved by a new gadget—wireless. Wireless operator Jack Binns sent out the first-ever S O S signal as an emergency request for assistance. Nearby ships responded, and the rest is history. Binns became a cult hero, and songs and poems were inspired by this man and his "supernatural powers." Unfortunately, it took the loss of over 1,500 people on the RMS *Titanic* before wireless operations and other safety features were extended internationally. *Treasure Island Museum (TIM)*

for. Owners often think they need a few more trips out of a hull that should have been allowed to rust into oblivion years ago, only to be left clueless when they founder. A ship founders when the hull plates come loose underwater or they simply have too many rust-potted holes that open up the flow of water. Multiple coats of paint to the water level might make the ship look seaworthy, but the hull and where the engine vibration impacts the most is what counts.

The SS *Britanis* foundered on October 21, 2000, off Cape Town, South Africa after decades of service to many lines. The SS *Sea Breeze I* foundered on December 17, 2000, off Cape Hatteras on the East Coast. These ships are excellent examples of vessels that had outlived their usefulness. The *Britanis* was going to be scrapped, and the *Sea Breeze I* was being towed for patchwork repair to squeeze a few more years out of the old ship. Both vessels are from a different age and pre-date hardwired automated systems. Of course, there are other vessels that were in much better shape and were lost at sea, such as the SS *Oceanos* of the Epirotiki Lines, on August 4, 1991. The vessel sank in a fierce storm off the coast of South Africa, and, fortunately, all of the passengers and crew were rescued. That was the third Greek cruise ship lost since 1989.

The Greek cargo vessel (former *Liberty* ship) SS *Kulukundis* ashore at Point Honda north of Santa Barbara, California, in the Devil's Jaw. The year was 1948, and the now demilitarized vessel grounded in a thick fog despite radar and a working fathometer. Seagoing tugs and salvage vessels, such as the *Salvage Chief,* quickly pulled the *Kulukundis* off the sandy beach, and an examination of the hull revealed only minor damage. *Author's collection*

Shifting sands and icebergs that take a new track in the gulf stream from the Labrador glaciers in the North Atlantic are always a problem. It was a series of icebergs that drifted further south than normal in 1912 that destroyed the *Titanic*. The *Titanic* and steamship SS *Arizona* (November 7, 1879) are two of many ships that hit icebergs and were disabled or sank. The SS *Hans Hedtoft* struck an iceberg on its maiden voyage and presumably sank on January 30, 1959. There were no survivors, few radio messages, and no recognizable debris. Icebergs are forever dangerous and always unforgiving.

The Graveyard of the Pacific is located at the mouth of the Columbia River where it empties into the Pacific Ocean. There are similar ship graveyards all over the world, such as on the Skeleton Coast in Africa and Point Honda (also known as the Devil's Jaw) just north of Santa Barbara, California. Cape Hatteras on the East Coast, Sable Island, and a number of coastal areas on the European, northern Scottish, and Irish coasts also have claimed the lives of countless ships. Huge storms seem to congregate in these areas during the winter, and mariners avoid the areas if possible. Cruise ships will never be found in these areas except in the few

The SS *Catalina* is grounded for perhaps its final time in February 2002. The *Catalina*, once a familiar sight steaming between Los Angeles Harbor and Avalon on the leeward coast of Catalina Island, now sits on the bottom of Ensenada Harbor in Baja California, Mexico. The steamer is 285 feet in length with a 52-foot beam, and was driven by a triple-expansion steam engine. From her early beginning in 1924, the vessel has had ties to Southern California. Her present condition in the backwaters of a foreign port makes it probable that the *Catalina* will soon be just a memory. *Author's collection*

The *Mary D. Hume* rots away in an area adjacent to the Rogue River in Gold Beach, Oregon, in July 2002. She was once a powerful oceangoing tug that pulled the largest of vessels to their moorings. There was one futile attempt to preserve this page of nautical history, but it failed. Soon, the *Mary D. Hume* will disappear into the wind and waves. *Author's collection*

weeks of each year when rescuers can be reasonably assured that inclement weather will not occur.

The ever-changing composition of sandbars and entrances to major rivers are another threat to mariners. The Columbia River is a perfect example of an area where millions of gallons of water flow out of the river each minute that change the entrance almost daily, yet, large vessels have to transverse this area to get to Portland, Oregon. Constant dredging and continued observation by the U.S. Coast Guard occur to ensure the sea lanes are kept open and safe.

Storms account for many ships being lost, especially those that are of the inter-island variety and should not be at sea when wind and wave are active. Over the last several years, there has been a large number of ferry boats that ply between islands in Third-World countries where airfare is too high, there are no airfields, and travelers outnumber aircraft. Unfortunately, many of these ferry boats have low freeboard, low speed, and are overcrowded. In any sea state beyond dead calm, doom and death follow these ships. Foundering, capsizing, and even

The RMS *Titanic* barely slides by the SS *New York* (right) as it leaves the Port of Southampton, England, on the first day of its maiden voyage in April 1912. The suction of its giant propellers pulled the smaller steamship *New York* away from its moorings and snapped the mooring lines. As can be seen, a collision was barely averted, some say through the skill of Captain Smith of the *Titanic* when he nudged the ship to a higher speed. Others say responsive tugs in the immediate area rushed to push the new liner out of harm's way. *TIM*

The liner SS *America* burns at a Newport News Shipyard dock in Virginia on March 10, 1926. This vessel, owned by United States Lines, was being refurbished and overhauled. The fire spread quickly in the 23-year-old ship and steam-powered fire pumps (bottom left) were used to fight the fire. The blaze was not terrible enough to prevent the ship from being saved, and it was used for an additional 30 more years. Shipyard fires are common due to the abundance of hazardous materials found there. *TIM*

swamping occur, and hundreds, if not thousands, of innocent passengers are killed. Often, there are few traces of these ships because the territory's coast guard isn't equipped to assist the sinking vessels or rescue the potential survivors.

Squalls can come up in minutes, and before a crew can batten down its hatches and warn passengers, significant damage can occur. Winds of up to 60 miles per hour and heavy wave action can threaten even the most seaworthy and largest cruise ships. This is now more true than ever, as cruise ships are built with so much superstructure exposed to act like a sail, which makes them more difficult to maneuver in strong weather conditions.

Ships themselves can cause accidents. A large vessel with powerful engines can move down a narrow channel and literally pull another vessel into its wake or its side. On April 10, 1912, as the *Titanic* left her berth in Southampton, England, the suction of her outboard props pulled the American liner SS *New York* away from her moorings and nearly caused a collision. The pull was so strong the mooring hawsers snapped like twigs. The officers and men responsible for the *Titanic* were uncertain as to the level of power the props commanded. In concert with the collision with an unanticipated iceberg, this ignorance played a significant role in the death of the *Titanic* a few days later.

This car ferry travels from Tangiers, Morocco, to Algerciras, Spain, daily. The lifeboat davits are rusted shut, the fire hoses are rotting, and the life jackets are difficult to locate. It is doubtful that the radar works, and the officers pay little attention to the route and ships passing because the ship makes the trip every day. A fully loaded gasoline tanker came within 100 yards of the ferry in February 2003, yet neither slowed their pace. *Author's collection*

Man-Made or Assisted Factors

There is an old saying that the captain of a ship is the "master after God." In this day of instantaneous communication, that concept is somewhat mitigated and outmoded. However, the power of a captain is undeniable. The person with the attractive uniform with four stripes who hosts the captain's cocktail party on a cruise can make life or death decisions about the welfare of the crew and passengers under his or her control. In lieu of the captain, the officer of the deck acts in place of the commanding officer and has full power. Turning a ship one way or another can result in life or death for the ship, its crew, its passengers, and perhaps those of another ship. There are other man-made difficulties at sea that can be as bad or worse than what the sea or related elements can throw at a ship. In the case of warships, there are explosives and nuclear power to contend with, as well as operating in close quarters.

Incompetence on the deck or in the engineering department can result in a ship running aground or engine failure at a crucial moment. Laziness, drunkenness, and drug use can result in difficulties for passengers and crews. Also, for anyone who has spent any length of time at sea, it is easy to become complacent. Fire hoses, valves, and boat davits should be checked, repaired, and replaced when necessary. They are often just painted over to make them appear operational. Multiple coats of paint over rusted surfaces also increases the risk of fire in the

The U.S. Coast Guard buoy-tender *Aspen* (WI B-208) moored at Yerba Buena Island in the San Francisco Bay in August 2002. This new 225-foot tender and two of its sisters, the *Spar* and the U. S. Coast Guard tender *Cypress,* have experienced engine room fires that have been traced to human error rather than equipment failure. The problems have been corrected, but even on the finest vessels staffed with the most highly trained technicians, fires and explosions can occur in the engine rooms and other areas.
Author's collection

An OSCAR II (NATO code name)-class guided missile submarine plows through the water with its blunt nose. The SSGN *Kursk,* or *K-141,* was laid down in 1992, launched in 1994, and commissioned a year later. The task of the *Kursk* and its fellow OSCAR II boats was simple—kill NATO or U.S. Navy carrier battle groups or destroy coastal cities with nuclear guided missiles. Primarily, the OSCARs were to be the underseas nemesis to the surface battle groups that might threaten Russia. The *Kursk* sank in the Barents Sea on August 12, 2000. There were no survivors, and few clues were left behind to determine the cause of death.
Author's collection

The former tanker USS *Ponaganset* (AO-86) broke in half on December 9, 1947. The 523-foot long, 22,380-ton vessel fully loaded was demilitarized and being converted for commercial use when it fractured. Several ships that were hurriedly built during World War II (primarily *Liberty* ships) experienced difficulties that were similar, and a few were lost without a trace. Of course, this is just a supposition, but many mariners point the finger to shabby construction and poor welding. *TIM*

area. Fires can spread quickly aboard a vessel, and they often begin in engine rooms, where combustible materials are abundant.

Carelessness also plays a part in inadequate ship maintenance and repair. Whether it is when the ship is in dry dock for overhaul or in regard to routine work at sea, some crew members do not do a good job and simply hope for the best. Perhaps that frayed wiring or chafed rope will never present a problem, but when it does, lives can be lost. All of the causes for accidents, injury, damage, and death that occur ashore have added problems when one is at sea.

Neglecting important duties, such as repacking valves and making certain that engines are in good working order, can be extremely dangerous. When a fire main or a fuel cut-off valve is faulty in an emergency, the ship is put in real danger.

Such nonchalant care is somewhat mitigated by periodic checks and inspections by coast guards and other regulatory agencies, but even they cannot verify that everything is in order.

One of the attractions of taking a vacation on one of the many cruise lines is the fabulous array of food. How often have advertisers told us that everything is

The SS *Enchanted Capri* moored in New Orleans, Louisiana, in June 2001. This vessel was built in 1958 and was periodically updated. However, it may be part of a shipping company that cannot guarantee sailing dates and is recurrently laid up for financial or other reasons. According to locals, the *Enchanted Capri* had been laid up for quite a while, and its future was unclear. It is a shame to see a vessel of this caliber rust away in the backwaters. The *Enchanted Capri* displaces 23,395 tons and is capable of carrying 725 passengers. In June 2001, the U.S. Coast Guard denied requests to sail the *Enchanted Capri* due to safety concerns. These types of vessels generally have no real ports of call and offer what are known as "cruises to nowhere." *Author's collection*

included, and everyone will gain 6 to 10 pounds during a weeklong cruise? On average, a large cruise ship serves around 90,000 courses per day, not including the 24-hour limited grill and room service. Cruise lines have taken institutional feeding to a whole new height of success, but with it comes the occasional problem. Virtually all cruise vessels have foreign-registry ports, such as Panama, Liberia, and the Bahamas. The United States has certain watchdog agencies, such as the National Transportation Safety Board (NTSB), the U.S. Coast Guard, and the Centers for Disease Control and Prevention (CDC), to inspect ships that cruise out or into U.S. ports. Unfortunately, the $12 billion annual income cruise industry escapes most corporate taxation, and it looks the other way when it comes to labor laws, security,

and the environment. Of course, the United States' war on terrorism has put new scrutiny on all transportation, and cruise lines are not able to dodge these issues as they once did on a wholesale basis.

The U.S. Coast Guard has duties to ensure shipboard safety standards are met, and it provides rescue services as needed. The NTSB investigates and provides answers to questions about how and why a vessel, its crew, and passengers are at hazard. The National Oceanic and Atmospheric Administration (NOAA) becomes involved when ships and nature interact in ways that are potentially unsafe to ecosystems.

The CDC became involved in the regulatory picture when the number of ships carrying passengers from U.S. ports increased in the late 1960s and

Posted Missing

BERGE ISTRA

early 1970s. A Vessel Sanitation Program was instituted and formalized, which calls for two annual unannounced inspections aboard all ships that serve food. Ships are graded and must earn 86 points out of 100 to retain their certification and the right to serve food. The process has been quite successful, as the number of major problems has dropped from 12 to 15 incidents per year in the 1970s and 1980s to 3 or less per year today. Lately, though, there has been a recent surge of scares, such as the 260 cases of severe food poisoning aboard the cruise ship *Disney Magic* in June 2000. However, inspections and the threat of government sanction have improved cleanliness aboard ships, especially in food preparation areas.

Aside from direct causes that are manmade or assisted, some poorly built ships break up under pressure at sea, sometimes without any apparent reason. For example, the former U.S. Navy oil tanker the USS *Ponaganset* (AO-86) was surveyed out of the navy in 1947 and was to be rebuilt by private interests. Unluckily, on December 9, 1947, in Boston Harbor, the demilitarized tanker split right down the middle to the keel. This rendered the ship useless, and it was soon scrapped. In the rush of wartime construction, something went wrong, and the hull was unable to sustain the stresses of construction.

Aside from mechanical, engineering, and safety-equipment maintenance aboard ship, poor financial management can also affect a ship. Bankruptcy can cause one to be laid up for long periods of time, and it requires a lot of attention to bring a ship back to normal operating condition.

Unfortunately, there are shipping companies that operate on a shoestring budget and stretch the life of older vessels beyond what is safe. These companies are often just one-ship companies, and if the vessel is not at sea continuously, the money coffers are not filled. Deferred maintenance takes a back seat to slim profit making, and the ship slowly deteriorates.

Unexplained and Mysterious Factors

There are hundreds of thousands of vessels plying the world's oceans, seas, rivers, and inland waterways. It is not unusual for ships to disappear without a trace. In the days before the wireless telegraph and other forms of electronic tracking, ships disappeared on a regular basis. Today, vessel accountability is far greater and easier, but ships still occasionally disappear.

Perhaps the largest of all vessels in terms of raw tonnage to be lost at sea was the Norwegian ore/oil carrier M/V *Berge Istra*. This ship, a 223,963-ton supertanker, had a wing tank explode just forward of its bridge on December 30, 1970. Thirty members of its 32-man crew were lost as the ship quickly disappeared into the Mindanao Trench, near the Philippine Islands, which is approximately 34,000 feet deep. Two Spanish crew men were rescued by the Japanese fishing boat *Hachiho Maru Number Six* after they spent 19 days on a life raft that drifted several hundred miles from the sinking. The ship was carrying 188,000 tons of iron ore from Brazil.

A year after the *Berge Istra*, the 8,196-ton M/V *Banaluna* reported its position as 1,000 miles from Kokura, Japan, carrying a full load of magnetite iron concentrate. The date was November 9, 1971, and that was the last contact from this vessel.

The list of lost vessels is phenomenal, and its ships often had the same characteristic—they were carrying high-density cargo that shifted easily.

Piracy and Hijacking

To many, there is a certain degree of romance when it comes to piracy. We think in terms of "Long John Silver" or "Yo, ho, ho and a bottle of rum." The reality of it all is quite different. There is no romance, and the pirates are not handsome. However, they do like rum, as well as any alcohol or drug. In most cases, they do not have weapons more sophisticated than long-handled knives or cheap guns or rifles. Today's pirates are brutal and will steal anything that can be easily taken. Typically, they attack at night by crawling up the side of a vessel, whether at sea or in a harbor. The watch is overcome, and the vessel is taken over and looted. Items such as the crew's belongings, including clothing, money, and weapons, may be stolen, and the pirates disappear into the night. Often, the raids are foiled by alert and armed watch keepers. They sound the general alarm, which usually is enough to drive the pirates away. Generally, pirates are not so dedicated as to risk their lives for a few trinkets, so retreating is the better part of valor.

Occasionally, seize pirates do capture inter-island ferries, and after they steal everything, they kill the passengers and crew. The ships are sold to illegal brokers and rebuilt, repainted, and re-registered in

Opposite: A crude picture of the tanker M/V *Berge Istra,* the largest vessel to ever be posted "missing." It is surmised that the ship is at the bottom of the Mindanao Trench near Mindanao, Philippines, some 34,000 feet under the surface of the ocean. Two Spanish seamen who were painting the ship witnessed the explosion near the bridge aft, and the ship vanished underwater within minutes. Luckily, they made it to a raft, and although they drifted for days and hundreds of miles, they were saved. Another mystery of the sea. *Author's collection*

The British-built steamship SS *Haida* took to the water in 1909. Here, the 3,800-ton vessel is shown on October 22, 1937, in Seattle harbor. The *Haida* was sold to Chinese interests but retained its British flag. Two days later, she sailed from Seattle with a load of 5,000 tons of sulfur for China. The ship and her 45-man crew were never seen again. There were no wireless transmissions, and one theory is that Japanese agents in Seattle noted the *Haida*'s departure, and a Japanese I-boat (submarine) sank the old tramp steamer with torpedoes. That is just an educated guess based on the events taking place in the world, the ownership of the vessel, its cargo, and its destination. *Author's collection*

the backwaters of a harbor. However, most piracy centers on small boatloads of knife-wielding men who attempt to take over vessels, including large tankers and bulk carriers, and rob the crews and steal any portable cargo or ship fixtures.

Terrorism on the sea still exists, such as the attack on the American destroyer USS *Cole* in Aden Harbor, Yemen. A suicide attack very similar to the *Cole*'s took place on the French supertanker M/V *Limberg* on October 7, 2002, in the Gulf of Aden. The huge ship stayed afloat, but it burned viciously. Terrorism at sea will continue, and the most accurate guided missile is a boat or aircraft piloted by a zealous human against an unsuspecting target.

Barratry is a form of shipwrecking that was once quite popular. Barratry is wrongful or deliberate conduct that results in the loss or destruction of a vessel. This could mean deliberate grounding or collision with another ship or allowing a vessel to burn out of control. Insurance underwriters examine these types of losses carefully to determine if there is any form of barratry or if the owners are at fault in the loss of the vessel.

The reasons for ships being lost are many and diverse. Some losses will never be explained, yet, like all aspects of seafaring lore, a lost ship is most interesting when people gather around a fireplace with a raging storm outside.

CHAPTER 2

The HMS *Oceanic,* completed in 1899, was one of the vessels that started the White Star Line on its way to greatness. This vessel was built by the Harland and Wolff Shipyard in Belfast, Ireland, and had 17,274 gross tonnage. It was also 704 feet in length with a 68-foot beam. The *Oceanic* carried three classes of passengers (1,710 total), all in greater comfort than the more common cattle boats. The *Oceanic* was capable of 21 knots, and was the first liner to exceed the length of the SS *Great Eastern*, which held the record in steamer length for 40 years. Like so many vessels that were hastily requisitioned for wartime use in 1914, the *Oceanic*, now a merchant cruiser, piled up on the rocks off Foula Island near Scotland. The new merchant cruiser was commissioned on September 8, 1914, and weeks later in the Shetland Islands, the ship was stranded in dense fog on Foula Island. Fortunately, the entire crew of 400 officers and men were rescued, but the ship was declared a constructive loss. It took 10 years to fully break up the old ship. *TIM*

COLLISIONS

White Star Line

The White Star Line of 1912 shared something in common with the owners of the *Mayflower* of 1620. Both transported immigrants from Europe to the United States for a price. The 104-foot, 180-ton *Mayflower* carried 102 dissident churchgoers from England to the New World. The *Olympic* class (RMS *Olympic*, RMS *Titanic*, and HMHS *Britannic*) of ships displaced 46,328 tons (not fully loaded), or more than 257 times that of the *Mayflower*.

From the time North America was discovered, immigrants, mostly from Europe, flocked to its shores for a new life. Traffic was most pronounced from the mid-1850s through World War I. Selling the family home and farm often provided just enough money for the entire family, including grandmother, to travel aboard one of the many ships that sailed daily from England, Ireland, or France. Passengers mainly traveled on ships that were designed specifically for the immigrant trade. Some of the ships were so primitive that accommodations consisted only of a small allocated space in unheated, wet cargo holds, with common toilet facilities and bare subsistence-level food. The trip took anywhere from 5 to 30 days, provided the ship remained afloat and its engines did not fail. The ships were generally iron- or wooden-hulled steamers that plodded, rather than sailed, the Atlantic. Steel hulls and dependable engines appeared toward the end of the nineteenth century, as did many other improvements in ship design.

Shipping lines were much like late-twentieth-century airline companies. Many companies offered cut-rate fares. Governments did not regulate trade to the extent they do today, so savvy businesses saw to their own profit, and sometimes it was at the expense of competitors.

Crushing the life out of one's competitor was permissible and laudable. The White Star Line came to be and flourished in this atmosphere.

The White Star Line, founded in Liverpool in 1850, was the natural outgrowth of a company that had provided wooden-hull passenger/cargo service from Europe to Australia. Gold hunters were on their way to Northern California or Australia. The White Star Line mainly catered to those traveling to Australia. This particular route was immensely popular in the middle of the nineteenth century, and, in 1867, the line began to alter its perspective. The company made money, but indecent profit was the goal. That meant altering the route to the North Atlantic and the eastern United States. Thomas Ismay joined the company and guided the line toward the lucrative North Atlantic ferry business.

During the summer of 1907, new goals had to be established, or the company would slip behind its competitors. An ad hoc planning session quickly envisioned the construction of new ships at a minimum of 100 feet longer than their close rival, Cunard. Luxury beyond what was presently conceivable was the next absolute when building this type of ship. Speed was important, but not an overriding concern. The ships should be able to make at least 24 knots and be capable of 22 knots on a sustained basis.

A ship almost 900 feet long with a nearly 100-foot beam and displacing up to 50,000 tons would be impossible to build at Harland and Wolff's shipyard in Belfast, Ireland, without substantial modifications. High-capacity cranes and gantries and huge slips would have to be constructed. This grand ship idea was to be the *Olympic* class—the largest ships and man-movable objects in world history. The vision of three monster passenger ships dominating the world's oceans overrode

The *Cedric,* one of the White Star Line's "big four." The other ships were the *Celtic, Adriatic,* and *Baltic.* The ships were built and entered service around the turn of the twentieth century. Each became the largest and best as they entered service for the White Star Line. The *Cedric* and *Celtic* were 700 feet in length, 75 feet wide, and displaced 20,904 tons. They carried up to 2,847 passengers, including 2,350 in third class. As the race to build bigger and bulkier ships continued, small-ship owners expressed fear and concern about the recklessness and arrogance of the big steamship operators. More than a few smaller, coastwise vessels had been rammed or almost hit by big ships without regard for any safety concerns. *Author's collection*

conventional wisdom. On July 31, 1908, just over a year later, White Star initiated and signed a formal contract with Harland and Wolff to build the *Olympic*-class ships.

The *Olympic, Titanic,* and RMS *Gigantic* were larger-than-life symbols of a much more significant philosophical issue in the early years of the twentieth century. Man was now capable, or so it seemed, of limitless visions and the mental capacity and drive to create anything that could be conceived. Ideas that were once only fanciful dreams could be turned into reality. Man could fly in heavier-than-air machines, electricity doubled the potential work time of factories and industry, and the telephone and Marconi's wireless systems broke down geographical barriers. Ships were able to reach over 20 knots on a sustained basis and were continuously being improved from a safety standpoint. Unfortunately, it was ship safety rather than passenger safety that was stressed.

RMS Olympic

The *Olympic* was launched on October 20, 1910, and was fitted out for service by May 1911. The sliding ways for the launch were 772 feet in length and required 22 tons of tallow to be smeared on the timbers to enable the vessel to have a smooth ride from dry land to water. It was important for the *Olympic* to enter service as soon as possible to bring in revenue to the shipping line.

The *Olympic* had a lucrative mail contract, hence the Royal Mail Ship (RMS) prefix, but the immigrant trade made the difference. The ships still relied upon passenger trade and were known as floating palaces because of the plush nature of their fittings and the "highbrow" art and other pieces of sculpture found onboard. The *Olympic* class carried up to 1,034 passengers in first class, 510 in second class, and 1,022 in third or steerage class. The shipping lines attempted to move away from the

Nº 92295

THIRD CLASS

Male Berth ..✓.........
Female Berth ....
Married Berth ....

WHITE STAR LINE

ROYAL AND UNITED STATES MAIL STEAMERS

ISMAY, IMRIE & CO.,
COOKSPUR STREET, SW.
NR. LEADENHALL STREET, EC.
LONDON.
JAMES STREET
LIVERPOOL
GANUTE ROAD, SOUTHAMPTON

Agent at PARIS
NICHOLAS MARTIN, 9, Rue Scribe

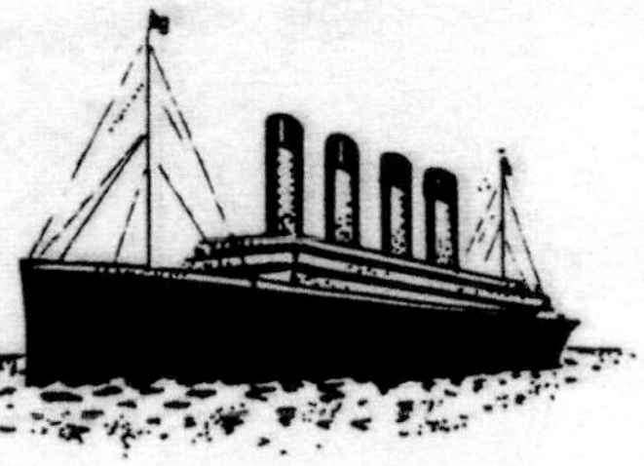

WHITE STAR LINE
18. VIA ALLA NUNZIATA .... GENOA
21. PIAZZA DELLA BORSA .... NAPLES
24. STATE STREET .... BOSTON
9. BROADWAY .... NEW YORK
53. DALHOUSE STREET .... QUEBEC
BELL TELEPHONE BUILDING
118. NOTRE DAM STREET WEST .... MONTREAL

JAMES SCOTT & CO. Agents
QUEENSTOWN

OCEANIC STEAM NAVIGATION COMPANY, LIMITED, OF GREAT BRITAIN.

THIRD CLASS (Steerage) PASSENGER'S CONTRACT TICKET
(NOT TRANSFERABLE).

1. jupe pour plus de sécurité (voir photo). Grande poche pour documents de voyage, chèques, billets, etc. Petite poche telephone
2. Ce portefeuille anti-vol s'attache à votre ceinture au moyen de deux passants et peut se rentrer à l'intéripantalon ou ne
3. Ce portefeuille anti-vol s'attache à votre ceinture au moyen de deux passants et peut se rentrer à l'intérieur de votre pantalon ou jupe pour plus de sécurité (voir photo). Grande poche pour documents de voyage, chèques, billets, etc. Petite poche pour cartes de crédit et pièces. Ref. 2 lephonegedragen worden voor extra veiligheid (zie fotos). Te gebruiken voor reisdocumenten, cheques, geld,
4. Verborgen Portefeuille wordt aan uw riem bevestigd d.m.v. twee lussen en kan aan de binnenzijde van uw broek of rok gedragen worden voor extra veiligheid (zie fotos). Te gebruiken voor reisdocumenten, cheques, geld, kreditkaarten, etc.
5. Ce portefeuille anti-vol s'attache à votre ceinture au moyen de deux passants et peut se rentrer à l'intérieur de votre pantalon ou jupe pour plus de sécurité (voir photo). Grande poche pour documents de
6. De Verborgen Portefeuille De veiligste anti-diefstal portefeuille ter wereld. Gemaakt van zacht en soepel leer. De
7. e portefeuille anti-vol s'attache à votre ceinture au moyen de deux passants et peut se rentrer à l'intérieur de votre pantalon ou jupe pour plus de sécurité (voir photo). Grande poche pour documents de De Verborgen Portefeuille De veiligste anti-diefstal portefeuille ter wereld. Gemaakt van zacht en soepel leer. De
7. A telephone telephone telephone telephone telephone telephone telephone telephone telephone telephone telephone telephone telephone telephone telephone telephone telephone

SHIP *TITANIC* of *46,328* Tons Register
to take in Passengers at LIVERPOOL *for* NEW YORK.

NAMES	AGES	Equal to statute to Adults
OLAF GUNDERSEN	19	

Deposit .... 2 .... £
Balance .... £
Total .... 12 – .. £

Deposit deposit Deposit Deposit deposit Deposit

Portefeuille Anti-Vol Le portefeuille anti-vol le plus sûr au monde! Matière: cuir souple d'excellente qualit
Ce portefeuille anti-vol s'attache à votre ceinture au moyen de deux passants et peut se rentrer à l'intérieur de votre pantalon ou jupe pour plus de sécurité (voir photo). Grande poche pour documents de voyage, chèques, billets, etc. Petite poche pour cartes de crédit et pièces. Ref. 2
De Verborgen Portefeuille De veiligste anti-diefstal portefeuille ter wereld. Gemaakt van zacht en soepel leer. De Verborgen Portefeuille wordt aan uw riem bevestigd d.m.v. twee lussen en kan aan de binnenzijde van uw broek of rok gedragen worden voor extra veiligheid (zie fotos). Te gebruiken voor reisdocumenten, cheques, geld, kreditka

Teuille Anti-Vol Le portefeuille anti-vol le plus sûr au monde! Matière: cuir souple d'excellente qualit
Ce portefeuille anti-vol s'attache à votre ceinture au moyen de deux passants et peut se rentrer à l'intéripantalon ou jupe pour plus de sécurité (voir photo). Grande poche pour documents de voyage, chèques, billets, etc. Petite poche pour cartes de crédit et pièces. Ref. 2
De Verborgen Portefeuille De veiligste anti-diefstal portefeuille ter wereld. Gemaakt van zacht en soepel leer. De Verborgen Portefeuille wordt aan uw riem bevestigd d.m.v. twee lussen en kan aan de binnenzijde van uw broek of rok gedragen worden voor extra veiligheid (zie fotos). Te gebruiken voor reisdocumenten, cheques, geld,
Fefeuille Anti-Vol Le portefeuille anti-vol le plus sûr au monde! Matière: cuir souple d'excellente qualit
Ce portefeuille anti-vol s'attache à votre ceinture au moyen de deux passants et peut se rentrer à l'intérieur de votre pantalon ou jupe pour plus de sécurité (voir photo). Grande poche pour documents de voyage, chèques, billets, etc. Petite poche pour cartes de crédit et pièces. Ref. 2
De Verborgen Portefeuille De veiligste anti-diefstal portefeuille ter wereld. Gemaakt van zacht en soepel leer. De Verborgen Portefeuille wordt aan uw riem bevestigd d.m.v. twee lussen en kan aan de binnenzijde van uw broek of rok gedragen worden voor extra veiligheid (zie fotos). Te gebruiken voor reisdocumenten, cheques, geld, kreditkaarten, etc.

BILL OF FARE

gedragen worden voor extra veiligheid (zie fotos). Te gebruiken voor reisdocumenten, cheques, geld,
Fefeuille Anti-Vol Le portefeuille anti-vol le plus sûr au monde! Matière: cuir souple d'excellente qualit
Ce portefeuille anti-vol s'attache à votre ceinture au moyen de deux passants et peut se rentrer à l'intérieur de votre pantalon ou jupe pour plus de sécurité (voir photo). Grande poche pour documents de voyage, chèques, billets, etc. Petite poche pour cartes de crédit et pièces. Ref. 2
De Verborgen Portefeuille De veiligste anti-diefstal portefeuille ter wereld. Gemaakt van zacht en soepel leer. De Verborgen Portefeuille wordt aan uw riem bevestigd d.m.v. twee lussen en kan aan de binnenzijde van uw broek of ro gedragen worden voor extra veiligheid (zie fotos). Te gebruiken voor reisdocumenten, cheques, geld, kreditkaarten, etc.Ce portefeuille anti-vol s'attache à votre ceinture au moyen de deux passants et peut se rentrer à l'intéripantalon ou jupe pour plus de sécurité (voir photo). Grande poche pour documents de voyage, chèques, billets, etc. Petite poche

JOSEPH BRUCE ISMAY
telephone telephone

A replica of a third-class ticket for the *Titanic*. The same type of ticket was used for other vessels. It is interesting to see the large number of interlocking companies that are involved in the shipping line. *Author's collection*

The RMS *Olympic* slides down the 772-foot siding ways that have been greased with 22 tons of tallow and liberal amounts of grease. The date is October 20, 1910, and the ship must now go to a fitting-out berth for final preparations. The *Olympic* was completed on May 31, 1911—four years after the leaders of the White Star Line envisioned the largest passenger ships in the world. *Courtesy Ulster Folk and Transport Museum*

The RMS *Olympic* slowly steams near the Harland and Wolff Shipyard. In the far background, the gantry with the RMS *Titanic* under construction can be seen. The *Olympic* has just been removed from its outfitting dock at the shipyard, and this photograph gives quite a panoramic view of the size of the shipyard. *Courtesy Ulster Folk and Transport Museum*

The bow of the scout cruiser HMS *Hawke*. This 7,350-ton displacement cruiser was 387 feet in length and was reasonably well armed. It mounted two 9.2-inch guns; ten 6-inch; twelve 6-pounders; and had four 18-inch torpedo tubes submerged in the hull. The *Hawke* carried 544 officers and men and could reach 20 knots (coal-fired triple-expansion) on 12,000 horsepower. The cruiser steamed down Spithead Channel and was drawn into the suction of the RMS *Olympic*'s power and disparity in displacement. The little cruiser smashed into the starboard side of the *Olympic*. The *Olympic* was found at fault, and the *Hawke* was repaired. As a matter of interest, the *Hawke* was lost to a torpedo on October 15, 1914, that was fired by a *U-9*, a German submarine. There were 524 lives lost out of 544 crew members. *Author's collection*

The RMS *Olympic* at sea after its hull was painted black. It now resembled the RMS *Titanic*, and, as usual, there is no smoke from the fourth stack. That stack is fake and used only for storage. The White Star Line placed it on the *Olympic* class to take advantage of the myth that the more stacks, the more powerful and safer a vessel. The loss of the *Titanic* put an end to that belief. *Courtesy Ulster Folk and Transport Museum*

The damage to the RMS *Olympic* from the collision with the HMS *Hawke* on September 20, 1911. The *Olympic* was holed in two locations 80 feet from the stern. Although the damage was not mortal to either ship, it required a return to a dockyard for repair for both. Note the two workmen in the bottom right of the image. *Courtesy Ulster Folk and Transport Museum*

term "steerage," because it conjured up the old-fashioned cattle boat image, and third class had a slightly better image.

The *Olympic* had a 945-member crew that included 75 in the deck force (officers and medical department), 326 in the engineering department (engineers, oilers, and stokers), and 544 hotel staff (food service, stewards, and nannies).

The *Olympic* was the twelfth vessel in the White Star Line, which in 1911 included 29 other steamers and tenders in its overall ownership plus a sail-powered training vessel. In the second decade of the twentieth century, it was certainly the largest vessel, at 45,324 tons with an 892-foot length and a 92-foot beam. Like its two sisters to follow (*Titanic* and *Britannic*), the new ship was driven by a powerplant that consisted of two four-cylinder reciprocating engines that drove the two wing propellers as well as a center-mounted low-pressure turbine engine that drove the center propeller. The turbine engine was fed by steam runoff from the reciprocating engines and created up to 16,000 horsepower, while the two reciprocating engines produced up to 17,000 horsepower. With all boilers (29 massive maws that consumed some hand-fed 600 tons per day) online and a maximum effort from the black gang (engineering staff), the ship could press up to 24 knots for short periods. Of course, this meant that fuel usage was massive and highly uneconomical, which defeated the entire purpose of the engine arrangement. One major flaw

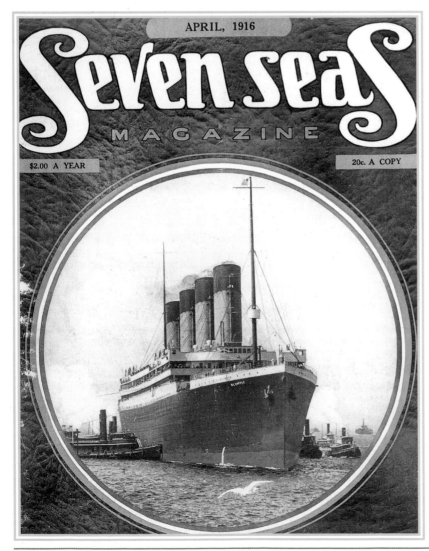

APRIL, 1916

Seven seas
MAGAZINE

$2.00 A YEAR

20c. A COPY

Seven Seas Magazine was distributed by the Navy League of the United States in the early 1900s. This cover features the steamship RMS *Olympic* and a bevy of tugboats as they leave a harbor. *Author's collection*

WHITE
STAR
LINE

R.M.S. "OLYMPIC." 46.
(The largest British Stea
Viewed from a Seaplane whilst on Wa

The RMS *Olympic* in its battle, or dazzle, colors. The former passenger liner now is what is known as a trooper, and a closer look shows two surface 6-inch guns aft. Those weapons are more for show than anything else. As the war wound down, the *Olympic* used her bow as a weapon when she struck and sank a U-boat that had attempted to torpedo her. *TIM*

in this system that haunted the *Titanic* was that the center-mounted turbine engine had no reverse gear. This, combined with a small rudder for such a large vessel, spelled doom for quick maneuvering. In the case of the *Titanic*, when the iceberg was sighted several hundred yards away, there was absolutely no hope to avoid a collision. To a degree, the fault was built into the design.

The first voyage of the *Olympic* was from Southampton, England, to New York. Her average outward speed was 21.17 knots. Capt. Edward J. "E.J." Smith, soon to be commodore of the White Star Line, was in command. The *Olympic* was the largest man-made object ever built, and the port authorities in New York were stunned when they watched this behemoth glide into harbor. Up to this point, nothing had occurred to mar the reputation of the *Olympic*, but as 12 small harbor tugs pushed the monster to its mooring, the *Olympic* reversed its starboard propeller and pulled the tug *O.L. Hallenbeck* against the hull. The 1/2- to 3/4-inch-thick steel hull plating of the *Olympic* was more than an even match for the wooden tug, and the *Hallenbeck* was critically damaged during the encounter. Financial amends were made, the liner embarked passengers for the Old World, and it sailed back to Great Britain. All in all, the trip had been a public relations triumph.

Three months later, another accident befell the *Olympic* and Captain Smith. As the *Olympic* passed down the Spithead Channel on September 20, 1911, at the allowable harbor speed of 19 knots, the HMS *Hawke*, a Royal Navy scout cruiser, was inadvertently pulled across 300 yards into the starboard side of the *Olympic*. The bow of the *Hawke* was crumpled back just forward of its bridge, and its forward gun emplacement was destroyed. The ruling was that the disparity in size and power of the ships caused

At the war's end, the RMS *Olympic* backs away from a pier with the assistance of a tug. The foremast shows the crow's-nest. It was the same as the *Titanic*'s. *TIM*

the smaller to be sucked into the side of the larger. The *Olympic* and White Star Line were found at fault. The *Olympic,* now with a black-painted hull, had two gashes—one above the water line and one below the water line, 80 feet from the stern. The ship had to offload its passengers and return to Harland and Wolff for repair, thus it delayed work on the next of the three, the *Titanic.* Smith was not found at fault because the *Olympic* was under the command of a harbor pilot at the time.

Five months went by before the *Olympic* suffered any additional mechanical or collision difficulties. In February 1912, the ship lost a propeller blade and had to return to Harland and Wolff for repair. The *Titanic* had to surrender one of its blades to the ailing *Olympic*. This, in turn, caused an additional three-month delay in introducing the *Titanic* to the North Atlantic run.

In early April 1912, the public seemed to forget about the *Olympic*. Among much fanfare and a huge media campaign, the *Titanic* had arrived. It was a few tons heavier, larger, and slightly more luxurious than the *Olympic*. After the *Titanic* foundered on April 15, 1912, the *Olympic* was about as popular as the bubonic plague, but people still had to travel.

The *Olympic* had two more scrapes with disaster before she met the scrapper's torch. It collided with the SS *Fort Hamilton* (formerly the SS *Bermudan*) of Furness Lines in 1924. No mortal damage was done, and little was said in the media because both vessels made it back to port under their own power.

In May 1934, the *Olympic* steamed into the USS *Nantucket,* a lightship stationed off the American coast. The *Nantucket* sunk in the thick fog and seven crew members were killed. The sole fault fell to the

The lightship *Chesapeake* is now a museum ship in Baltimore Harbor. The *Chesapeake* is very similar to the *Nantucket,* which was run over by the RMS *Olympic*. Most areas around lightships are now lit by towers with automated lighting. *Author's collection*

An artist's rendition of the collision between the RMS *Olympic* and the lightship *Nantucket* off the U.S. coastline. The lightships were there to report ship traffic and of ship locations. The *Olympic* hit the *Nantucket* in a dense fog and seven men were killed aboard the *Nantucket*. *TIM*

Olympic, and an indemnity of $500,000 had to be paid by the White Star Line to the families of the dead and to the government for the loss of its vessel.

On October 11, 1935, old reliable, the sole survivor of the once great *Olympic* class, began her last trip from Southampton.

RMS Titanic (1912)

The keel of the *Titanic* was laid next to the *Olympic,* which was under construction at Harland and Wolff, on March 31, 1909. On April 6, 1910, the ship was fully framed and the skeletal outline of the great ship began to take place.

The shell plating on the *Titanic* was completed on October 19, 1910, and the huge ship slid down the ways on May 31, 1911. Less than 11 months later, the first linens were spread on new tables. It was expected that the ship would sail for decades and ultimately end up in a scrap yard. In reality, a year later, the ship and everything in it was strewn over a 1/4-mile debris field 2-1/2 miles under the surface of the North Atlantic and would not emerge into daylight

until years later, when it was located on the ocean floor in 1985. The *Titanic,* the world's largest, most luxurious vessel at the time, only sailed a few hundred miles before it collided with an iceberg.

In a strange fete of prediction, Morgan Robertson wrote *The Wreck of the Titan Or, Futility.* It was copyrighted by M. F. Mansfield in 1898 and again by Morgan Robertson in 1912. The book is 243 pages long and contains four short fiction stories. The first is *The Wreck of the Titan Or, Futility,* and the other three are about pirates, American naval warships, and confused allegories to both. The account in the book is so realistic it is a near-psychic accident prediction of the loss of the *Titanic.*

Robertson's story was about the steamship the RMS *Titan,* the world's largest man-made object. Every contemporary element of science, profession, and trade had been employed in its construction. There were 19 watertight compartments that could be isolated in 30 seconds by turning a lever. The *Titan* was considered practically unsinkable. She was 800 feet in length, offered 70,000 tons of

The RMS *Olympic* takes her last voyage from Southampton to the scrap yard. She was the only one of the unlucky trio left, and she had given good service to her owners. Its age was against the old ship, and the upkeep was too expensive. This, along with a worldwide depression and shipping glut, meant it was time for the *Olympic* to be broken up. *Author's collection*

displacement, and could muster 75,000 horsepower to drive her at 25 knots. The *Titan* carried as few lifeboats as would be tolerated by the British Board of Trade. They were only to be used to row passengers to a rescue ship in the unlikely event the *Titan* would encounter unprecedented danger. The lifeboats carried a maximum of 500 people, and there were no rafts to interfere with the morning constitutional walks of first- and second-class passengers.

The *Titan*'s bow was reinforced with heavy steel to plow through harbor ice and small craft that might get in its way and interrupt "full-speed trade and delivery of the mail," as the vessel was contracted for. The ship would move at 21 knots or greater through fog, wind, waves, and storms.

Two or more days out of port, just after midnight, the ship was moving near full speed when its starboard side struck an iceberg. The ship slowly sank,

and hundreds of passengers and crew were lost. Survivors included the ship's owner and a few others who clung to their lives on the limited number of boats. There, the story trails off into a series of sidebar issues, but the similarities to the *Titanic* are astonishing, especially since this book was published 14 years before the foundering of the *Titanic* and at least a decade before the name of the ship and its rough particulars became known to the media and public.

The *Titanic* was 892 feet in length, offered 66,000 tons in full displacement and 55,000 horsepower, and had a maximum speed of 24.5 knots. It had 10 watertight compartments and carried the minimum number of lifeboats required by the British Board of Trade. Harland and Wolff strongly suggested a minimum of 48, and the builder, Thomas Andrews, asked for 64, but the White Star Line demanded and provided only 20.

The RMS *Titanic* as "cold iron"—no machinery and no life. It sits in the fitting-out basin at Harland and Wolff in Belfast, Ireland. Soon after, swarms of workers crawled all over the ship and brought it to life. *Courtesy Ulster Folk and Transport Museum*

The Wreck of the Titan Or, Futility sold less than 800 copies in 1898. Sales skyrocketed in 1912 and again in 1998 when the film *Titanic* hit movie theaters worldwide. For years, Morgan Robertson was considered an authentic psychic, but he chose to be known as a fictional maritime writer. His book about the *Titan* was merely an accident and was not inspired by some supernatural source.

RMS Titanic *and Reality*

On April 14, 1912, at 11:40 P.M., the world's largest and most luxurious ocean liner struck an estimated 800,000-ton iceberg in the North Atlantic 500 miles from land. The *Titanic*, the 66,000-ton pride of the White Star Line, struck the iceberg at 22.5 knots (25 miles per hour) and bumped along its starboard side for 300 feet (one-third of the liner's length). The damage was not immediately obvious, but, of course, it was inevitably lethal. In the next 2 hours and 40 minutes, 712 souls escaped in 20 lifeboats, which left behind 1,523 relatives, friends, and acquaintances. The actual number that remained aboard is still a mystery, because infants and stowaways were not included on the passenger manifests. At 2:20 A.M. on April 15, 1912, the "unsinkable" *Titanic* quietly disappeared beneath the 28-degree surface of the North Atlantic. Ten minutes later, the separated bow and stern sections completed their 2.5-mile journey to the ocean floor. By 2:40 A.M., there were no more pleas for help from those in the water, and all that could be heard were the muffled cries of the passengers in the lifeboats.

The RMS *Titanic* is led down a channel by a tug, as evidenced by the wake in the bow area of the great ship. For onlookers, this was an awe-inspiring sight. It was the world's largest man-made object to move through the water. *Courtesy Ulster Folk and Transport Museum*

CAPTAIN SMITH AND OFFICERS S.S. TITANIC.
Lost on 15th April, 1912, after collision with Iceberg in North Atlantic.

The officers of the RMS *Titanic*. The four striper is Capt. Edward J. Smith (known as the "millionaires captain" due to his popularity with the wealthy). To his right is Chief Officer H. F. Wilde. To the captain's left is First Officer William Murdock. Second Officer Charles Lightoller (with the rugged seaman's face, second from the top left) was also quite popular. There was some bitterness between Chief Officer Wilde and First Officer Murdock, because Murdock felt he should have been chief officer. *Courtesy Ulster Folk and Transport Museum*

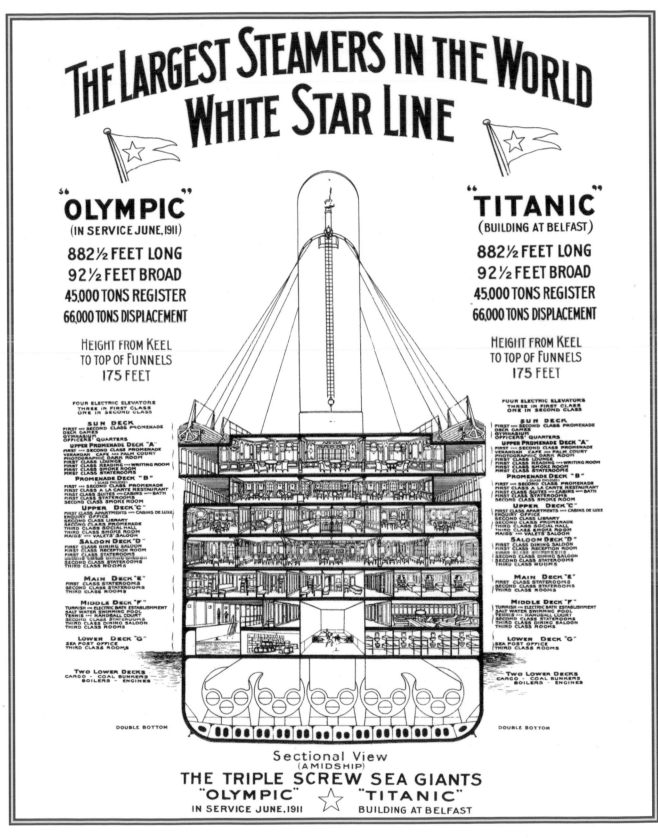

THE LARGEST STEAMERS IN THE WORLD
WHITE STAR LINE

"OLYMPIC"
(IN SERVICE JUNE, 1911)

882½ FEET LONG
92½ FEET BROAD
45,000 TONS REGISTER
66,000 TONS DISPLACEMENT

HEIGHT FROM KEEL
TO TOP OF FUNNELS
175 FEET

"TITANIC"
(BUILDING AT BELFAST)

882½ FEET LONG
92½ FEET BROAD
45,000 TONS REGISTER
66,000 TONS DISPLACEMENT

HEIGHT FROM KEEL
TO TOP OF FUNNELS
175 FEET

FOUR ELECTRIC ELEVATORS
THREE IN FIRST CLASS
ONE IN SECOND CLASS

SUN DECK
FIRST AND SECOND CLASS PROMENADE
DECK GAMES
GYMNASIUM
OFFICERS' QUARTERS
UPPER PROMENADE DECK "A"
FIRST AND SECOND CLASS PROMENADE
VERANDAH CAFE AND PALM COURT
PHOTOGRAPHIC DARK ROOM
FIRST CLASS READING AND WRITING ROOM
FIRST CLASS SMOKE ROOM
FIRST CLASS STATEROOMS
PROMENADE DECK "B"
(GLASS ENCLOSED)
FIRST AND SECOND CLASS PROMENADE
FIRST CLASS A LA CARTE RESTAURANT
FIRST CLASS SUITES AND CABINS WITH BATH
FIRST CLASS STATEROOMS
SECOND CLASS SMOKE ROOM
UPPER DECK "C"
FIRST CLASS APARTMENTS AND CABINS DE LUXE
ENQUIRY OFFICE
SECOND CLASS LIBRARY
SECOND CLASS PROMENADE
THIRD CLASS SOCIAL HALL
THIRD CLASS SMOKE ROOM
MAIDS' AND VALETS' SALOON
SALOON DECK "D"
FIRST CLASS DINING SALOON
FIRST CLASS RECEPTION ROOM
FIRST CLASS STATEROOMS
SECOND CLASS STATEROOMS
THIRD CLASS ROOMS
MAIN DECK "E"
FIRST CLASS STATEROOMS
SECOND CLASS STATEROOMS
THIRD CLASS ROOMS
MIDDLE DECK "F"
TURKISH AND ELECTRIC BATH ESTABLISHMENT
SALT WATER SWIMMING POOL
TENNIS AND HANDBALL COURT
SECOND CLASS STATEROOMS
THIRD CLASS DINING SALOON
THIRD CLASS ROOMS
LOWER DECK "G"
SEA POST OFFICE
THIRD CLASS ROOMS

TWO LOWER DECKS
CARGO - COAL BUNKERS
BOILERS - ENGINES

DOUBLE BOTTOM

FOUR ELECTRIC ELEVATORS
THREE IN FIRST CLASS
ONE IN SECOND CLASS

SUN DECK
FIRST AND SECOND CLASS PROMENADE
DECK GAMES
GYMNASIUM
OFFICERS' QUARTERS
UPPER PROMENADE DECK "A"
FIRST AND SECOND CLASS PROMENADE
VERANDAH CAFE AND PALM COURT
PHOTOGRAPHIC DARK ROOM
FIRST CLASS LOUNGE
FIRST CLASS READING AND WRITING ROOM
FIRST CLASS SMOKE ROOM
FIRST CLASS STATEROOMS
PROMENADE DECK "B"
FIRST AND SECOND CLASS PROMENADE
FIRST CLASS A LA CARTE RESTAURANT
FIRST CLASS SUITES AND CABINS WITH BATH
FIRST CLASS STATEROOMS
SECOND CLASS SMOKE ROOM
UPPER DECK "C"
FIRST CLASS APARTMENTS AND CABINS DE LUXE
ENQUIRY OFFICE
SECOND CLASS LIBRARY
SECOND CLASS PROMENADE
THIRD CLASS SOCIAL HALL
THIRD CLASS SMOKE ROOM
MAIDS' AND VALETS' SALOON
SALOON DECK "D"
FIRST CLASS DINING SALOON
FIRST CLASS RECEPTION ROOM
SECOND CLASS DINING SALOON
SECOND CLASS STATEROOMS
THIRD CLASS ROOMS
MAIN DECK "E"
FIRST CLASS STATEROOMS
SECOND CLASS STATEROOMS
THIRD CLASS ROOMS
MIDDLE DECK "F"
TURKISH AND ELECTRIC BATH ESTABLISHMENT
SALT WATER SWIMMING POOL
TENNIS AND HANDBALL COURT
SECOND CLASS STATEROOMS
THIRD CLASS DINING SALOON
THIRD CLASS ROOMS
LOWER DECK "G"
SEA POST OFFICE
THIRD CLASS ROOMS

TWO LOWER DECKS
CARGO - COAL BUNKERS
BOILERS - ENGINES

DOUBLE BOTTOM

Sectional View
(AMIDSHIP)
THE TRIPLE SCREW SEA GIANTS
"OLYMPIC" ☆ "TITANIC"
IN SERVICE JUNE, 1911   BUILDING AT BELFAST

A cutaway version of the RMS *Titanic* and its sister ship, the RMS *Olympic* shows the decks and particulars. *Author's collection*

Surveys 32.

SURVEY OF AN EMIGRANT SHIP.

BOARD OF TRADE, SURVEYORS OFFICE
No. HCR
13 APR. 1912
QUEENSTOWN

Issued by the
Board of Trade.

Certificate for Clearance.

Ship's Name and Official Number. (1.)	Port of Registry, and Tonnage. (2.)		Name of Master. (3.)
Titanic 131428	Liverpool Gross 46328	Register. 21831	E.J. Smith.

Port of Departure. (4.)	Ports of Call. (5.)	Destination. (6.)
Southampton	Cherbourg and Queenstown	New York

CABIN PASSENGERS.

Adults (12 years and upwards).				Children.				Total Cabin Passengers. (15.)	Equal to Adults computed by Part III. M. S. Act, 1894. (16.)
Married.		Single.		Between 1 and 12		Under 1 Year.			
Male. (7.)	Female. (8.)	Male. (9.)	Female. (10.)	Male. (11.)	Female. (12.)	Male. (13.)	Female. (14.)		
52 39	52 39	196 5	101 58	10 3	12 2	4		427 172	412½ 169½

STEERAGE PASSENGERS.*

Adults (12 years and upwards).				Children.				Total Steerage Passengers. (25.)	Equal to Adults computed by Part III. M. S. Act, 1894. (26.)
Married.		Single.		Between 1 and 12.		Under 1 Year.			
Male. (17.)	Female. (18.)	Male. (19.)	Female. (20.)	Male. (21.)	Female. (22.)	Male. (23.)	Female. (24.)		
25 4 5	25 4 2	315 59 56	71½ 13 54	22 4	28 3	3	3	495 182 113	464½ 92½ 110

CREW.

Deck Department. (27.)	Engine Department. (28.)	Stewards' Department. (29.)	Total Crew. (30.)	Equal to Adults computed by Part III. M. S. Act, 1894. (31.)
73	325	494	892	892

Total Number actually on board, including Crew	2208	2147

* Total Number of Statute Adults (as Steerage Passengers), exclusive of the Master, Crew, and Cabin Passengers, which the Ship can legally carry according to space allotted	Clear Space in Sq. Ft.	Number of Hoods fitted.
1735	26992	1134

I hereby certify that the particulars inserted in the above form are correct. I also certify that all the requirements of the Merchant Shipping Acts relating to emigrant ships, so far as they can be complied with before the departure of the ship, have been complied with, and that the ship is, in my opinion, seaworthy, in safe trim, and in all respects fit for her intended voyage ; that she does not carry a greater number of passengers than in the proportion of one statute adult to every five superficial feet of space clear for exercise on deck ; and that her passengers and crew are in a fit state to proceed.

61

Dated at Queenstown this 11th day of April 19 12

E.J. Sharpe
Emigration Officer, or Assistant Emigration Officer.

(238x) (02245) Wt. 30276/150 3000 12-10 W B & L

Certificate for Clearance issued that allowed the *Titanic* to sail with emigrant trade on April 11, 1912. It also certified the total number of people who left Ireland on the ship was 2,208. This may or may have not been accurate, depending on the number of stowaways and infants. *Author's collection*

This is probably the last photograph of the RMS *Titanic* as it left Queenstown, Ireland. The small boat in the lower right more than likely just removed the pilot from the great ship. This photo was taken shortly after 2:00 P.M. on April 11, 1912, with a Kodak Brownie camera by Frank Browne. *Courtesy Eddie J. O'Donnell SJ.*

The possibility of the lifeboats returning to the area where passengers were thrashing in the water was an almost universal and strange telepathic decision to avoid it until "things quieted down," according to survivors. Only four floating survivors were plucked from the below-freezing waters.

Just under two hours later, the speeding SS *Carpathia* came in amongst the lifeboats to rescue the survivors. The rescue ship hoisted 13 boats aboard, and, after an exhaustive search of the area that included seeing a huge iceberg with red paint residue, left for New York harbor.

This is an ice drift line as plotted in the 1935 edition of Bowditch's *American Practical Navigator*. The lowest line shows that ice drifted further south in 1912 than in any other year except for 1934. This accounts for large icebergs being where they were not expected. Captain Smith made the turn southward appropriately, but did not realize that ice was so far down the tract. He also ignored warnings by eastbound steamers that saw icebergs and flow ice at lower than usual regions for that time of year. *Author's collection*

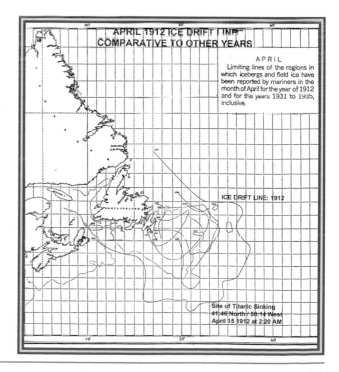

Ship of Dreams

In a rush to meet the April 10, 1912, sailing date, the *Titanic* was hastily outfitted and provisioned. Prophetically, 1,250 pounds of beluga caviar were brought aboard, but there were no binoculars for the lookouts. Her crew was conscripted from a variety of other ships and her commanding officer, Capt. Edward J. Smith, came directly to the *Titanic* from an assignment aboard her sister ship the *Olympic*. This was to be the 59-year-old Smith's last trip before retirement. He was going to go home to his wife and child and tend garden after 50 years at sea.

When the *Titanic* left Southampton for New York, she was the largest ship ever built. The *Titanic* represented technology at its finest and was proof that man now had conquered nature. At 66,000 tons full load, the 892-foot-long ship could accommodate more than 3,000 passengers and crew in comfort. Her first-class cabins commanded an estimated $50,000 (2003 dollars) one-way, yet, third or immigrant class sailed for less than $100. She carried just over 2,200 souls on her maiden voyage—899 were crew members and 710 were in third class. She burned 600 tons of hand-fed coal per day in her 159 furnaces to power the three engines, which could create up to 55,000 horsepower. As the trip unfolded,

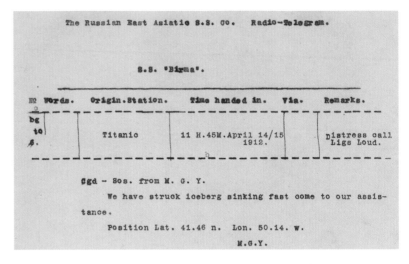

A copy of a wireless to the East Asiatic Steamship Company vessel SS *Birma* from the RMS *Titanic* (code name M.G.Y.): We have struck iceberg, sinking fast come to our assistance. Position Lat. 41.46 N Lon. 50.14 W. Time of message 11:45 April 14/15 1912. *Author's collection*

J. Bruce Ismay, the CEO of the White Star Line, continually chided Capt. Smith to increase speed, and by late April 14, 1912, the *Titanic* was steaming at a steady 22.5 knots with all boilers online. Its maximum speed was 24.5 knots, yet Capt. Smith was somewhat concerned about stressing the engineering plant this early in its life cycle.

More than a dozen ice warnings had been received by the *Titanic* as the watch changed at 10:00 P.M. Capt. Smith had earlier altered course to avoid any potential icebergs, yet he maintained full

The Leyland Line SS *Californian* was part of the International Mercantile Marine Family. This ship sat 10 miles on the other side of pack ice from the *Titanic* as the liner sank. The night was clear, and the *Californian*'s watch officer watched the great ship sink with all lights blazing, including eight white distress rockets. The *Californian* didn't respond because its radio was turned off and the operator had gone to bed. The crew on the *Californian* also presumed that the *Titanic* was communicating with another ship and then disappeared over the horizon instead of downward. *Author's collection*

speed. The sky was clear and the sea was like a mill pond. Any danger could be seen easily, and what the *Titanic* could not avoid, she would run over with her reinforced bow. To this point, the *Titanic* was performing better than anticipated with only minor difficulties. Two watch officers and a quartermaster were on the bridge, and two lookouts in the crow's-nest carefully searched the horizon despite the chilling temperatures.

"Iceberg, Right Ahead!"

At 11:39 P.M., lookout Frederick Fleet noticed that the view of the stars on the horizon was obstructed. Within seconds, he confirmed that a towering iceberg was in the direct path of the *Titanic* and it was bearing down at 7 yards per second. He rang the alarm bell three times and called the bridge. The disinterested voice of Sixth Officer James P. Moody asked, "What do you see?" The frightened lookout screamed in reply, "Iceberg, right ahead." First Officer Murdock quickly ordered "hard a'starboard," and he tried to reverse all three engines. It was impossible to reverse the turbine engines, though, so he stopped the center engine (low-pressure turbine), which substantially reduced rudder control. If the great ship had turned just a few more feet, perhaps she would have survived. A half minute before 11:40, five men watched in horror as the huge blue iceberg rose out of the darkness. This particular iceberg had drifted further south than most that year, and it was virtually invisible. Due to the mill-pond-like ocean conditions, there was no telltale phosphorescence from wave action at the base of the iceberg, which made it even more difficult to see. Add to that the crew's lack of binoculars, the frigid temperatures, and the 25-mile-per-hour wind in the eyes of lookouts with no eye protection, and the stage for disaster was set. Despite the handicaps, the lookouts saw the iceberg and collectively willed the ship to turn. The bow began to point away from danger within seconds before the collision. At 11:40, the *Titanic* seemed to bump and brush by the iceberg. Ten seconds later, it appeared over. The immensity of ship, its movement past the iceberg, and the obstruction's disappearance in the wake of the *Titanic* deceived the lookouts and officers, but not for long.

The watch officers were soon joined by Captain Smith as they watched the iceberg disappear in the *Titanic*'s wake. The ship drifted to a stop. An inspection of the damage was made, and within minutes, William Andrews, the ship's designer, informed Captain Smith that the ship had less than two hours to live. The hull had been fatally ruptured in a

An RMS *Titanic* lifeboat pulls alongside the SS *Carpathia* in the early morning of April 15, 1912, and disgorges its survivors—eventually 712 in all. The story unfolded, and then the SS *Californian* steamed up and asked what the problem was. The crew was informed but told that its assistance would not be needed. Some of the passengers had to be hoisted aboard in coal bags because they were so exhausted by the ordeal. *Author's collection*

The Evening Sun newspaper got it wrong, as the media often does in the early stages of a crisis. The later news would not be so cheerful. *Author's collection*

number of locations below the water line. The much heralded watertight door system would only temporarily delay the inevitable. Captain Smith, faced with the loss of his ship and eminent death, reluctantly ordered the lifeboats swung out and loaded with women and children first. The 20 boats had a maximum capacity of 1,178 persons, which meant that over a thousand people would be left behind. As it was, due to confusion and lack of information on boat capacity, only 712 survived. Two out of three passengers and crew died. One boat left the ship with only 12 people aboard, and many people complained about the cold and refused to board the boats.

S O S, S O S, C Q D, C Q D: "Titanic struck a berg and is sinking."

Titanic's Marconi wireless operators were the second (the first was operator Jack Binns aboard the SS *Republic*) to use the new call sign for danger, "S O S," in a series of desperate pleas for help. Finally, the *SS Carpathia*, the nearest vessel—

There are rusticles on the bow of the RMS *Titanic* as she rests on the ocean floor some 12,500 feet below the surface of the North Atlantic. Estimates are that the ship will disintegrate into nature within 200 to 500 years. *Author's collection*

The popular theory of why the RMS *Titanic* sank was that an iceberg sliced the ship open like a knife. In 1985, the truth as to why the great ship was lost was revealed. Several hundred small punctures, popped rivets, lost caulking, and inaccessible areas to plug the leaks were among the main culprits. The lack of damage control and poorly trained crew only exacerbated the situation. The overall design, including the watertight doors, did little to keep the ship afloat. All in all, the loss of the *Titanic* would be considered a complete system failure, and, today, the U.S. Coast Guard would not even allow a ship designed like this out of harbor, as it would be considered a deathtrap. *Author's collection*

it was 58 miles away—responded and began steaming at full power to aid the *Titanic*. Even with a maximum effort, her arrival time was not until 4:00 A.M., more than four hours after the *Titanic* struck the iceberg. The SS *Californian* was stopped for the night within 10 miles of the collision, but it did not maintain a 24-hour radio watch, and the operator had turned off the set minutes before the frantic calls for help hit the airwaves. The distress rockets were also ignored by the crew of the *Californian* as likely being White Star Line company signals. When the officer of the deck aboard the *Californian* saw the *Titanic* disappear, he incorrectly assumed that the vessel in the distance had steamed down over the horizon.

Lifeboats were launched sporadically and were often only partially filled. Women and children were loaded first, yet, many men found their way onto the boats. Some were cowardly, others were necessary as seamen. Molly Brown, a Denver mining queen, virtually

The RMS *Titanic,* or "stage one," as it's built in the 17,000,000-gallon shooting pond for the movie *Titanic.* The cost for the ship was $18 million. After the scene where the people wave good-bye to the *Titanic,* all of the city sets disappeared, the pond was filled from the Pacific Ocean (to the right), and a 40-foot black shroud was erected around the set to black out the background of Mexican villages. *Author's collection*

This is what twilight at sea must have looked like aboard the RMS *Titanic.* Taken just before sundown from the set of the movie *Titanic,* this photo shows smoke coming out of the number two and three stacks. Number four was a dummy and used only for storage. This looked so real from a distance, but for the film, it was made of plywood, tin, hot glue, paper, and anything else that would look good and hold together for a few weeks. I leaned against one of the white engine room ventilators (deep background) and fell over with it. It was made of lightweight plastic and hadn't been glued to the deck. *Author's collection*

assumed command of boat number six, and her brusque personality probably saved some of the boat's occupants from freezing to death. Many third- or immigrant-class passengers never made it to a lifeboat for one reason or another. Most of the engine room staff perished at their stations. They maintained power until the end and are the tragedy's often unsung heroes.

Shortly after 2:00 A.M., all remaining boats were launched and pulled away from the ship. The *Titanic* began her death tilt as the orchestra played "Nearer My God to Thee." Suddenly, at 2:17, the ship started to break apart and the stern rose above the water, exposing the three propellers and rudder. People were now jumping or falling off the ship into the below-freezing water. At 2:20, the ship foundered. Many had to jump 90 or more feet into the water, which would have been like hitting concrete.

Within four to six minutes, the cries of the people in the water ceased. They all died from shock, hypothermia, fear, or froze to death. Only 300 bodies were found by a ship sent to recover them days later.

A large bounty was offered for the body of John Jacob Astor by his family, which was one of the richest families in the world. His body was found and identified by the $2,500 he kept in his coat pocket. The 300 found were huddled together about 25 miles from the collision site. The other 1,200 bodies either went down with the ship or drifted away.

The 712 survivors were rescued by the *Carpathia* and began their journey to New York. Thousands of anguished people waited for news and the *Carpathia* to arrive in New York Harbor. There were investigations and studies to determine the cause of the disaster. The owners and operators were formally found blameless by everyone except the public, yet, in the end, the sea had stalked the *Titanic*. The *Titanic* was created out of arrogance, and a chunk of ice provided a reality check. In the annals of the twentieth century, the loss of the *Titanic* became the most famous of all shipwrecks, and it may hold that position for decades to come.

Why Did the RMS *Titanic* Sink?

For decades, psychics, underwater explorers, metallurgists, historians, movie directors, and approximately 10 million amateur *Titanic* experts have offered opinions and the "real" truth about why the *Titanic* went down. The best answer I read was by the chief of the U.S. Navy's Bureau of Navigation: "The *Titanic* filled with water, and, as steel is heavier than water, it sank." It is rather simplistic, but this hits the mark closer than theories that proclaim that high or low sulfur content of the steel, poor workmanship, sabotage, aliens, or that it was actually the *Olympic* that sank and all of the nameplates were changed. The one rationale that was accepted until the *Titanic* was located on the ocean floor in 1985 was that a spur from the iceberg sliced the ship open. For decades, few stopped to think that steel cuts ice and not the other way around, or ice picks would be made of ice!

As the *Titanic* filming progressed, the "ship" or "stage one" was slowly reduced in size to appear as if it were sinking. The set was repaired during the day, and just before dark, the 17,000,000-gallon shooting tank was filled with seawater for the night's film shoot. By this point in the film schedule, the ship had settled so low in the water that the foremast with the crow's-nest was bolted to the ground. The rest of the ship rested in a 40- to 50-foot trench that was filled with water. Add 2,000 actors, extras, 20 lifeboats, distress rockets, and ice, and you have the RMS *Titanic* disaster. *Author's collection*

The infamous "poop deck" or "tiltarotor" from the movie set of *Titanic*. This entire section of the mock-up RMS *Titanic* could be lifted off by a heavy-duty crane and attached to a tiltarotor that would tilt the poop deck at a 90-degree angle and dump passengers into a pool of rather filthy water—water that eventually filled with Coke cans, cigarettes, and other objectionable items. The stunt people who were used in these scenes became intimately familiar with this device and literally loathed it. Luckily, there were few injuries and no deaths. *Author's collection*

The true answer lies in two separate areas. First, the issue must be viewed logically and then through the eyes of a historian with mechanical and maritime knowledge. Actually, only a small amount of mechanical and maritime knowledge is needed. Clues were given by First Officer Murdock and the limitations of the engineering plant:

The rudder was center mounted and too small for such a large vessel. The turning radius of the ship was too large. Avoiding small hazards even at some distance is nearly impossible given the cumbersome size of the *Olympic* class.

The center-mounted engine was a low-powered, low-pressure turbine that didn't have a reverse gear. It either moved forward or stopped. The officers who were transferred to the *Titanic* from other vessels in the White Star family were generally unfamiliar with the mega-large ships in the *Olympic* class and were especially not proficient with the operating limitations of the turbine powerplant. The officers on the bridge (Officer of the Deck William Murdock, Sixth Officer James P. Moody) were raised in sail, educated in triple expansion power, and had just become accustomed to turbine power.

The iceberg was approximately 800,000 tons in displacement, and 80 to 90 percent of it was underwater.

There was no wave action and no wash against the base that would alert the lookouts to its existence. It was also most likely a blue berg and clear. This would make it nearly invisible at long range.

The two lookouts did not have any binoculars because there were only enough for the officers. The status symbol of the binoculars was more important than the lookouts being prepared to see a few hundred yards further out to sea.

The vessel was traveling at 22.5 knots on all boilers. Although there was no natural wind, the wind-chill factor generated by the ship's speed was approximately

The James Cameron SS *Carpathia* in Mexico built for the movie *Titanic*. The tall mast structure is a rainmaker. Cameron felt it would be more dramatic to have the *Carpathia* enter New York Harbor in a rainstorm, so there was a big generated rainstorm. *Author's collection*

minus-5 degrees Fahrenheit. The lookouts had little warmth, no eye protection, and the icy wind in their eyes caused tearing and often required them to duck behind the crow's-nest shield for warmth. Despite a clear night, the ability to see great distances was difficult at best.

At approximately 11:39 P.M. on April 14, 1912, an 800,000-ton iceberg came into sight and the *Titanic* was steaming directly toward it at 7 yards per second. Hitting it straight on would have meant complete destruction of the ship, the loss of the majority of the passengers and crew, and almost immediate foundering. The lookouts spotted it at approximately 11:39:05 and rung the ship's alarm bell three times. Sixth Officer Moody answered the bridge phone and notified First Officer Murdock, who was already taking action.

First Officer Murdock reversed the wing engines full back, stopped the turbine engine, and had the pilothouse wheel turned to starboard, which turned the ship to port and away from the iceberg.

The end result was that the ship brushed against the iceberg for a distance of 300 feet, 20 feet under the water line, from just under the forward well deck to where the ship's hull straightened out. The damage was in a perfect location, and if someone had drawn a red line with "Hit Me Here" written in this area, he couldn't have found a more vulnerable region to mortally wound the great ship. Rivets popped, caulking split open, and plates were pushed in. The collision took 10 seconds, and it was 65 seconds from the moment the iceberg was sighted until the ship was mortally wounded. There was no effective damage control, and the ship had 160 minutes to live. First Officer Murdock's action to immobilize his two assets to control the ship (power and rudder control) removed any hope of saving the ship. Had he boosted the power and swung the ship to port, then it is probable that she would have not hit so hard, may have survived longer, and rescue ships could have saved everyone. At the least, there would have been a fighting chance for the *Titanic* to live through the night.

As it was, the largest vessel in the world slid under the quiet water at 2:20 A.M. on April 15, 1912, after it broke into two major pieces. The 2.5-mile journey to the bottom took 10 minutes. It is ironic that it took years to conceive, finance, build, and outfit such a vessel and just minutes to destroy it.

The *Titanic* was indeed the ship of dreams, and there were some major changes in the wake of its disaster: better safety at sea for us all, the International Ice Patrol, and a realization that everyone is entitled to the same treatment when it comes to safety issues aboard ships are a few. In addition, radio watches are now maintained on a 24-hour basis.

U.S. Senate hearings were held and resulted in more than 1,000 pages of testimony. A similar examination was conducted by the British Board of Trade. No fault was actually found, although J. Bruce Ismay, CEO of the White Star Line and titular head of the International Mercantile Marine, was soon referred to as J. "Brute" Ismay and retired to a private life in the countryside.

The loss of the *Titanic* was the beginning of the end of the White Star Line. Within two years, the world was at war, and many of its ships would be conscripted into the fight, including the *Olympic* and the *Britannic*. Ultimately, the White Star Line flag was hauled down in 1958. It had been flown up to that time almost as a courtesy by Cunard, which assumed control during the Great Depression.

Hollywood Versus Reality

"I worship the ground you have stomped me on." — Kit Bonner to James Cameron, Director, Titanic

Nine decades after the White Star Line steamship *Titanic* sank in the North Atlantic, interest in the ship and its tragic loss continues unabated. The latest among the dozens of productions depicting this tragedy is a film directed by James Cameron. The brief career of *Titanic* has assumed a near-mythical quality, and it ranks with some of the major phenomenona of the twentieth century. Theologians, philosophers, politicians, and nearly everyone who is familiar with the event has offered an opinion as to the timeless value of the *Titanic*.

Similar to the real *Titanic*, the movie of the same name has become the most expensive film to date, and the financial return has justified its expense. Cameron, director of *True Lies* and *Terminator*,

spared no expense or effort in making the *Titanic* as real on screen as it was in 1912. This film became the most expensive and biggest production in cinema history. It starred Leonardo DiCaprio, Kate Winslet, Billy Zane, Bill Paxton, and Academy Award winner Kathy Bates as Molly Brown. The real star of the show, however, was the 750-foot, $18 million replica of the doomed liner that sat in a 6-acre, 17,000,000-gallon pond. Cameron's standing instructions were that the *Titanic* replica was to be called a ship, and while onstage, you were aboard ship. If an employee called it anything else, he or she was history! Cameron was entirely focused on the completion of the film and making it as accurate as possible. He would not tolerate substandard work nor people who were not fanatical about doing the best job possible. Many people left the production and swore they would never work for him again. Frankly, I had great respect for his talent and dedication to the project. His people skills need some work, but he is in the business of making movies that are successful, and being hard-nosed is what it takes to succeed.

Due to the fact that I am over 50 years old, have white, thinning hair, and am somewhat corpulent, many of the younger actors and workers assumed that I was a *Titanic* survivor. After protesting 40 or 50 times, I gave up and told those who asked that it was bitterly cold on April 14, 1912, and I escaped in boat number six with Molly Brown. No one did the math, and I became something of a *Titanic* "Yoda."

Production began in September 1995 when Cameron and company dove to the real wreck of the *Titanic*, which lies some 12,378 feet beneath the surface of the North Atlantic. The M/V *Keldysh*, a Russian research ship, was chartered for the use of its two deepwater submersibles, the *MIR 1* and *MIR 2*. Interestingly, they were employed to examine the *Kursk*, the sunken Russian guided missile submarine, five years later.

To film the actual wreck of the *Titanic*, Cameron equipped one of the mini-subs with intense lighting systems and the other with a camera. He used a 35-millimeter camera modified for use at a depth that produces 6,000 pounds of pressure per square inch. Thousands of feet of film were shot of the wreck during 12 dives. Each trip down cost over $100,000. Unfortunately, as the North Atlantic filming segment was completed, person or persons still unknown laced the cast and crew's farewell dinner with drugs. No one was permanently injured, but a few became violently ill.

The bridge of the RMS *Olympic*. This was the only photograph the *Titanic* film's art department had to use to design for the ship's bridge.

The colorized bridge of the RMS *Titanic*. There were very few controls except for a wheel, engine room telegraphs, and a compass. It was a standing joke that the closest thing to a morgue was the bridge of a White Star Line vessel. There was no chitchat, and the only conversation was business. *Author's collection*

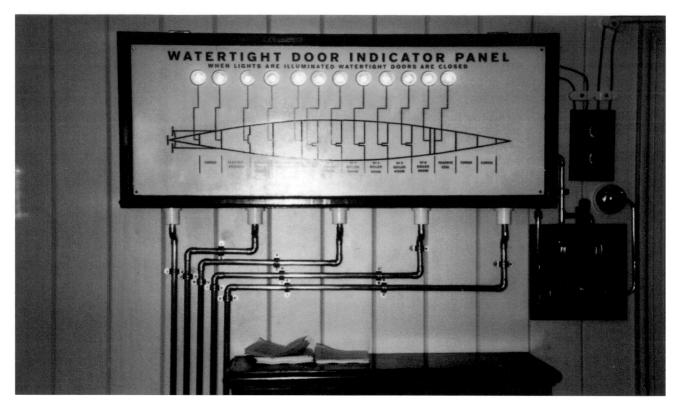

Hollywood's rendition of the watertight indicator panel for all compartments aboard the RMS *Titanic*. To the right is a button that had to be held down to begin the watertight door closing, which took about 25 seconds. In the film, it took 7 seconds, because 25 seconds would have been too long for the audience to wait. *Author's collection*

The RMS Titanic *Replica Makes Port in Rosarito Beach, Baja California, Mexico*

Next, it was time to build the biggest man-made shooting tank in the world. Various locations were considered, but Rosarito Beach, Baja California, Mexico, was selected. Just south of the Baja California resort city, a 40-acre beachfront site was purchased and construction began. A complete self-contained studio was built, including offices, indoor sets, and the seawater pond for the *Titanic* replica. As soon as the pond was completed, work began on the *Titanic* replica. Over a million feet of scaffolding interspersed with hydraulic lifts was erected to

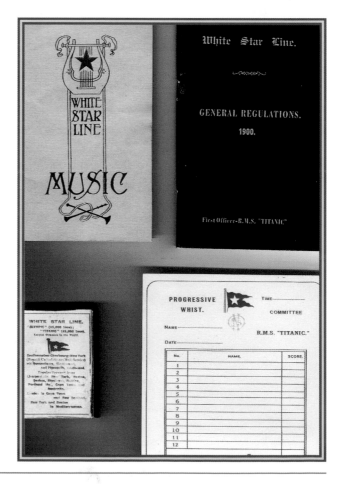

These are four items created from originals by the *Titanic* film's art department for use by the actors and actresses. The music book had 300 songs that a first- or second-class passenger could ask the orchestra to play. To the right is a booklet with White Star Line regulations, which was provided for the lifeboat drill each Sunday. April 14, 1912, was a Sunday. There is a matchbook cover and a *Progressive Whist* scorecard (similar to bridge). It cost $1 per day to rent a steamer blanket. *Author's collection*

The Soviet cruise liner M/V *Maxim Gorky* was built more than 40 years ago. After a rather checkered career of being owned and operated by a number of European shipping lines, the *Maxim Gorky* was reminiscent of the RMS *Titanic* in that it rammed into thick pack ice, on June 28, 1989. The damage was sufficient enough to warrant a complete evacuation of all passengers, but the ship did not sink. She was patched and towed to Murmansk for repairs. There have been smaller vessels that challenged the ice and are lost, but nothing has been on the same scale as the *Titanic*. It is unfortunate that lessons are not learned except through experience for some mariners. *Author's collection*

support a half-ship replica of the *Titanic*. From a nearby toll road, it looked as if a huge ocean liner had run aground. This often resulted in fender benders as people stopped to gawk at this oddity on the Baja coast. A secondary deep pool with a massive hydraulic tilt was erected to tip the poop deck for additional action shots of the ship in its final agonizing stages. Many actors were selected to fall from the poop deck to a variety of horrible deaths. At first, they believed they were special, but after floating in a fetid pool night after night, the luster wore thin.

In another sound stage, an indoor set, fully supported by hydraulically operated cables and straps, was built in a deep concrete tank. This set was of the ship's dining room, various interior passageways, and the first-class grand staircase. The interior of the ship had to sink as well as the exterior. Watching a stunningly beautiful dining room complete with 500 place settings of real china and silverware be destroyed time and time again was heart-wrenching. Out of consideration for the actors and shooting crew, the thousands of gallons of water in the tank were heated to 75 degrees. This caused a sauna-like effect, but it was preferable to ice-cold seawater.

In mid-November 1996, hundreds of "British-looking" extras, many of whom were Mexican nationals, assembled in 1912-period costumes to see the *Titanic* replica "sail." Many were loaded on a massive wheeled platform and waved farewell. The platform was hand pushed alongside the ship to simulate sailing.

The RMS *Britannic* on the ways of Great Gantry at Harland and Wolff in Belfast, Ireland. Note the scaffolding and the ramp for workers to get from deck to deck on the exterior of the ship. The hull has been painted, and a close look forward under the fourth port light shows the beginning of the name: *Britannic*. This vessel is already several thousand tons heavier in net displacement due to changes made as the result of the loss of the RMS *Titanic. Courtesy Ulster Folk and Transport Museum*

After the "ship" sailed, it was time to fill the huge pond to capacity. The pond, ranged in depth from 1 foot to 40 feet and was on the starboard side of the ship. The real Pacific Ocean was on the port side. The detachable bow was pointed toward San Diego. With the exception of Mexican fishing boats that sped back and forth off the coast directly in front of the studio, it looked remarkably authentic. An offer to pay boat owners $20 each to stay out of camera range brought an entire fleet of everything that could float the next day. Arrangements were made with Mexican officials, and the intruders soon disappeared. It was an easy task with coastal tankers and various cruise ships that could not resist the urge to come in for a closer look. A panoramic scene with the *Titanic* replica slashing through the ocean would certainly have been spoiled by a Carnival Cruise Lines Fun Ship in the background. Seagulls also presented problems. They swarmed around a makeshift trash dump located just off the *Titanic*'s

replica bow. A scene supposedly 1,000 miles at sea with seagulls flying around the ship was not acceptable. A junior production assistant was dispatched to chase the birds away.

Seagulls and speedboats were not the only nosy visitors. Security was intense to prevent media investigation and unauthorized photographs of the site and sets. In reality, the greatest concentration of pocket cameras was on the set. Every worker—there were some 7,500 overall—took clandestine photos. From time to time, security officers confiscated cameras and threatened dire consequences to the owners. Of course, the security officers also had cameras. Numerous attempts were made by news teams to infiltrate the studio, and many simply used telephoto equipment from a nearby hill that overlooked the complex. On occasion, a disgruntled extra provided inside information, though the credibility of the interview was always suspect. One television news team claimed that the *Titanic* replica would be used for a theme park or hotel casino in Las Vegas after the film was completed. Their vantage point did not include the port or ocean side, which was open scaffolding. If they had known the *Titanic* replica was constructed of plywood, pressed board, and aluminum supported by scaffolding, they would not have been so quick to predict its future. A passing rainstorm nearly destroyed the set before it could be sunk. Many of the deck planks buckled and the entire ship had to be squeegeed. Extensive repair work was necessary before shooting could resume.

From time to time, a helicopter would fly over the set and circle the *Titanic* replica for a good look. One night, while test firing distress rockets onboard the ship, an erratic rocket went several hundred feet in the air and exploded near an inquisitive San Diego news helicopter. The indignant occupants were eventually convinced that there had been no attempt to shoot them down.

Filming a major motion picture with hundreds of extras drowning, dying, swimming, screaming, and yelling is not an easy accomplishment. Exact-replica lifeboats were lowered 70 feet to the water many times, and credit is due to the actors and extras who spent night after night sitting in the boats, dangling above the surface of the pond while a revised lighting system was installed. Maintaining a sense of drama during the long hours of waiting taxed even the most seasoned professionals. During one highly complicated scene where the life boats are rowed from the dying liner amidst anguish and horror, with distress rockets exploding above, two workers calmly strolled across the pond, oblivious to what was happening. They

The launch of the RMS *Britannic* at Belfast, Ireland, on February 14, 1914, just six months before World War I began. It took more than 15,000 men to build this ship, and Harland and Wolff was a major employer in the area. The ship rides high because she has not been fully fitted out. When complete, it will come down to the water line. *Courtesy Ulster Folk and Transport Museum*

WHITE STAR LINE · R·M·S·BRITANNIC

A cutaway of what the RMS *Britannic* would look like if it had been completed as a passenger ship. Long before its completion as a liner, the vessel was refitted as the largest hospital ship in the world. The outlandish lifeboat davits can be seen aft. That worked when the ship was sunk in the Aegean Sea. *Courtesy Ulster Folk and Transport Museum*

were told to get out of "my [expletive] ocean." This was only matched by the vision of a first-class passenger picking his nose in the background of one scene. Keeping 1,000 people focused was very difficult for the production crew and resulted in an epidemic of heartburn.

The days became weeks, the weeks became months, and it was finally time to sink what was left of the deteriorating set. Everyone had anxiously awaited witnessing the *Titanic*'s replica plunge beneath the water surface. At first, everything seemed to work fine. The sun was shining, everyone was happy, and 1,000,000 pounds of hydraulic pressure on the cables holding the forward part of the ship, now known as the "riser," was set. The riser was lowered on a test basis, but it would not resurface despite all efforts. One of the cable brackets that was embedded in the bottom of the concrete pond had accidentally broken loose. Ironically, an $8 million New York musical *Titanic* had the opposite problem. Their *Titanic* would not sink!

Eventually, Cameron's *Titanic* replica worked fine and was sunk several times. The New York musical's set also began to work and now sinks nightly. With the climactic sinking of the *Titanic* replica complete, filming of was, of course, finished. The film was released in December 1997. It has grossed nearly $3 billion worldwide, and it is the world's top-grossing film. It has

The RMS *Britannic* (left) being outfitted as a hospital ship was one of the more strange images of the war. The ship is the old SS *Michigan* covered with planking to resemble the HMS *Collingwood*, as seen from the stern of the SS *City of Oxford*, which was rebuilt as the HMS *St. Vincent*. The idea was to secure a number of older commercial vessels that could be rebuilt as battleships, battlecruisers, or cruiser replicas to fool the enemy. It was a good idea that only partially worked. The men of the Special Services Squadron hoped they would never encounter anything stronger than a rowboat with bad intentions. *Courtesy Ulster Folk and Transport Museum*

The new HMHS *Britannic* as it was fitted out at Harland and Wolff. Alongside the conscripted hospital ship are two dummy battleships of the Special Services Squadron. The ships in the Special Services Squadron were somewhat close in size to the actual warships. This is an excellent comparison of the relative size of the *Britannic* to other vessels of the day. The RMS *Olympic* is in the background. *Courtesy Ulster Folk and Transport Museum*

The starboard profile of HMHS *Britannic* in 1916 before it was lost in November of that year. Note the extremely large flag flying from the foremast with a red cross on a white background. Everything that could be done to indicate that this ship was a hospital ship and noncombatant was done by the Admiralty. Likewise, belligerent nations did the same so that Allied ships, submarines, and aircraft would take a "hands-off" policy. Unfortunately, a mine does not recognize a red cross, thus there is greater chance the ship will be struck by a mine than a torpedo. *Courtesy Ulster Folk and Transport Museum*

been translated into many languages and is still playing as a first-run film in Taiwan.

Cameron's obsession with detail and accuracy created the most photo-realistic freeze-frame of this subject matter ever attempted. Historical accuracy was foremost in this effort, and even White Star Line score pads for card games were faithfully re-created. The uniforms fitted for the officers were based on the patterns, down to the gold-dipped buttons, which were provided by a tailor in London who had them stored from the days of the White Star Line. The uniforms with the gold insignias were valued at $5,000 during the shooting of the film, and they now command five times that amount. The carpet in the film was an exact replica of the *Titanic*'s. Exact replicas of Marconigrams

Another smaller hospital ship, the HMHS *Dover Castle*, was torpedoed and hit twice on May 16, 1917, near Gibraltar. The *Dover Castle* was in company with another hospital ship, the HMHS *Karapara*, and two destroyers when it was struck by the torpedoes. Prior to World War I, the 8,271-ton, 490-foot-long *Dover Castle* was popular as a passenger vessel after it entered service with the Union Castle Line in 1904. *Author's collection*

The HMHS *Lanfranc* was once a 6,287-ton, 433-foot-long steamer in the Booth Line in 1907. Here it is shown sinking stern-first, where it was struck by two torpedoes on April 17, 1917. The enemy submarine was driven off by destroyers and armed trawlers in the English Channel. The SS *Lanfranc* was converted to a hospital ship at the outbreak of World War I and was carrying Allied and German wounded to Southampton, England, on the day it was hit. Thirty-four of the 576 patients, crew, and medical staff perished, but 542 were rescued by naval escorts. The ship went down, and the explosions and damages were horrific, but maritime professionals learned about damage control and manning boats without panic. *Author's collection*

The now-decommissioned Alameda Naval Air Station in January 2001. The USS *Greeneville* (SSN-772) is in San Francisco for a port visit. The boat was being used as a test platform for the new Advanced SEAL Delivery System (ASDS) being tested at Pearl Harbor. Three weeks later, the ill-fated submarine struck and sank the M/V *Ehime Maru* in Hawaiian waters. *Author's collection*

(wireless telegraph messages) were used, and the emblem of the White Star Line was carefully engraved on the silver cutlery. Nothing has ever been attempted on this scale in cinema history. With the exception that the characters in the love story did not exist, only few minor mistakes were made, yet, only one was pointed out: When the ship turned over its propellers, all three began at once. This was incorrect. The center propeller was fed by a low-pressure turbine that was dependent on steam runoff from the two wing engines. The center propeller would have begun turning over after the two wing screws. In the 126,000 E-mail messages I received commenting on the accuracy of the film, only one marine engineer pointed that out. Most of the E-mail messages centered on whether the main

character, Rose, was still living and where she lived. Many people did not believe me when I wrote back that she was fictional and named after James Cameron's grandmother.

Most of the *Titanic* movie set was torn down and burned, including the deck chairs and life belts. Fortunately, as the naval consultant, I was allowed to bring home some artifacts, including dishes and engine room telegraph plates. What wasn't destroyed was taken as souvenirs. The engine was actually the *Liberty* ship SS *Jeremiah O'Brien*, which is located in San Francisco as a museum ship from World War II. It provided the vertical triple expansion engine for the engine room scenes. That, combined with an excellent art department, made the audience think they were deep in the bowels of

An emergency ballast blow performed by a now-decommissioned *Los Angeles*-class submarine, the USS *Birmingham* (SSN-695). The *Birmingham* was assigned to Pearl Harbor, and this manuever is what the *USS Greenville* was performing when it struck the M/V *Ehime Maru*. As the submarine ascended to the surface, rudder mortally damaged the underside, or keel area, of the Japanese school ship. *U.S. Navy*

Titanic's great engineering plant. The boilers were made of plywood, plastic, and sheet tin. Movie magic was everywhere, but on the other hand, the on-screen production and its realism is what counts.

HMHS Britannic (1916)

The plans of mice and men always seem to veer away from what was intended. The third vessel of the *Olympic* class, ostensibly to be named the *Gigantic*, probably would have been the most lavish and luxurious of all three ships. The White Star Line and Harland and Wolff would have learned from their experiences with the two prior giants they put to sea. World War I and the loss of the *Titanic* put an end to any immediate plans for the *Gigantic*, and the name was changed to the *Britannic*.

The keel of the *Britannic* was laid on the ways at Harland and Wolff in November 1911, and the partially completed ship was launched on February 26, 1914. War clouds were forming over Europe, and it was a matter of time before Great Britain was in a shooting conflict with the Central Powers led by Kaiser Wilhelm of Imperial Germany.

The *Britannic* was built with a double hull as a reminder of the loss of the *Titanic*, and it had a sufficient number of lifeboats for all. The machinery to accommodate the double hull and the new davits pushed the net tonnage to 48,158, far more than that of its predecessors, and it was bound to exceed 70,000 tons fully loaded. The *Britannic* would have become the largest of the three ships in the *Olympic* class. The White Star Line and every other passenger line of note was haunted with the loss of the *Titanic*, and anything and everything that could be done to install safety apparatus was included and heavily advertised. Safety had not been a real selling point for travelers before, but now it was. The lifeboat davits aft were huge and engineering marvels. Advertising booklets spoke of the wonders of the new lifeboat davits and the safety issues that had been addressed in the construction of the *Britannic*.

The *Britannic* enclosed the well deck and added a fourth main elevator for passenger convenience. Had this vessel ever been able to take to the North Atlantic sea lanes, it would have been a marvel and quite popular, but a war no one counted on intervened.

The USS *Greeneville* in dry dock at the Pearl Harbor Naval Shipyard as it is examined by shipyard technicians and National Transportation Safety Board officials. Just opposite the sail on the port side, damage is evident from the impact of the M/V *Ehime Maru*. *U.S. Navy*

The accommodations aboard the ship were for 2,500 passengers and 950 crew, and as the interior of the ship was being fitted with thousands of feet of mahogany and oak paneling, word came down that the Admiralty was going to requisition the liner as a hospital ship. On November 15, 1915, the Admiralty announced the *Britannic* would become His Majesty's Hospital Ship (HMHS) *Britannic*. To convert the ship to a hospital ship, most of the décor, art, and paneling had to be removed just a week after Harland and Wolff had delivered the ship on December 8, 1915. The ship was painted white except for buff-colored funnels, masts, and the international signs of a hospital ship—a green stripe mid-hull for the length of the ship punctuated by three red crosses. A rectangular red-background sign with the white letters "G618" was just under the bridge windows, and there were two large red crosses on the hull near the boat deck on each side of the ship. The huge boat davits and the ventilators on deck were also buff colored.

The life of the *Britannic* was short. Under the command of Capt. Charles Bartlett, the huge hospital ship was sunk in the Kea Channel within 55 minutes after it was hit by a torpedo or struck a mine at 8:12 A.M. on November 21, 1916. The explosion ripped the ship open between the number two and three holds on the starboard side forward, not far from where the *Titanic* suffered its lethal damage.

At approximately 9:07 on a bright sunny morning, with boats rowing ashore, the largest vessel in the British Merchant Marine rolled over on her beam ends and slipped below the water. All that was left was a floating debris field. The 55 minutes the *Britannic* did stay afloat were put to good use, as Captain Bartlett attempted to steer his wounded ship to a point of land a mere 2 miles away and lowered boats filled with wounded British soldiers, hospital staff, and the ship's crew. All but 30 of the 1,100 total aboard were saved, and 45 were wounded. Most of the boats got away safely, although the majority of the deaths occurred when one of the boats was trapped under a turning propeller.

The M/V *C-Commando* was chartered by the U.S. Navy to assist in locating the M/V *Ehime Maru*. The remote-controlled vehicle ROV *Scorpio II* was deployed from the *C-Commando* and sent back photos of the stricken vessel that showed it upright in the muddy silt bottom. *U.S. Navy*

The survivors made it to shore and were rescued. For the next 60 years, the wreck laid on its starboard side with a fissure across the entire hull just forward of the cargo derricks in front of the bridge. No one mounted a serious exploration of the wreck site until 1976.

Exploring the Wreck

In 1976, Capt. Jacques-Yves Cousteau was looking for the lost City of Atlantis in the Aegean Sea when he was asked by the *Titanic* Historical Society to find the *Britannic.* Cousteau agreed, and he located the ship about 400 feet below the surface and was able take several photographs. Another expedition occurred in September 1995, headed by Robert Ballard, who led the expedition to discover the *Titanic* in 1985. Several more images were taken with modern cameras, and the U.S. Navy's *NR-1,* a nuclear deep-submergence craft, was used.

The probable cause of the explosion was that the *Britannic* struck a mine. German U-boats didn't attack hospital ships until the later months of the war, and the *Britannic* was sunk in 1916. Many hospital ships were sunk by mines and torpedoes, but what is most important about this disaster is that so many men and women were saved in such a short period of time.

USS Greeneville (SSN-772) and the M/V Ehime Maru (2001)

The year 2001 was marked by one of the most high-profile maritime disasters of recent history. No large ships were involved, there was no threat to the environment, and only a limited number of people were killed. The high degree of initial and continued interest lies with the parties involved and the complete absence of any reasoning, other than carelessness, for the accident. On February 9, 2001, the U.S. Navy nuclear submarine USS *Greeneville* (SSN-772) surfaced at 1:43 P.M. during a routine emergency main ballast tank blow. In the process, the M/V *Ehime Maru* was struck. The commercial

Japanese vessel was owned and operated by the Uwajima Fishery High School. There were no injuries or deaths aboard the *Greeneville,* but 9 were killed out of the 35 students, teachers, and crew of the *Ehime Maru.*

The *Greeneville* was operating in or near the U.S. Navy's older restricted sea area off Pearl Harbor, Hawaii, and the *Ehime Maru* was instructing students in fish culture and habits in the same general vicinity. The U.S. Navy's submarine test and trial area had been developed decades ago for American submarines that come out of the Pearl Harbor Naval Shipyard to examine changes and updates, especially to make deep dives and test-fire torpedoes. The area is still marked on charts as a Notice to Mariners, but it is not considered a forbidden zone. U.S. submarines operate in this area, but it is no longer their sole turf. The test and trial area is opposite of Honolulu, and it begins at least 2 miles out to sea in a rectangular shape from the Honolulu Harbor side of the Honolulu International Airport to Diamond Head and then continues many miles out to sea.

The Vessels

The USS *Greeneville* (SSN-772) is an improved *Los Angeles*–class nuclear attack submarine. All *Los Angeles*–class submarines built since the USS *San Jose* (SSN-751) have been considered improved *Los Angeles*–class boats, or 688Is, and it was anticipated the *Greeneville* would be operational for at least 33 years. The 6,330-ton surfaced/7,177-ton submerged submarine is 109.73 meters in length, has a 10.06-meter beam, and was commissioned on February 16, 1996, in Norfolk, Virginia. In April 1997, the new boat, which has an operating depth of 450 meters, was transferred to the Pacific Fleet.

The *Greeneville* has the latest in electronic capability and can launch Tomahawk missiles and mines. This boat, as well as the newer *Los Angeles*–class boats, is built capable of cruising in the Arctic. The *Greeneville* was especially improved to carry out Navy SEAL operations by being a launch vehicle for the Advanced SEAL Delivery System (ASDS). The *Virginia* class, the follow-up class to the *Los Angeles*–class boats, has a minimum of five boats modified to

A televised scene of the bow of the M/V *Ehime Maru* from one of the remote-controlled vehicles. *U.S. Navy*

carry the ASDS, beginning with the USS *Hawaii* (SSN-776). The ASDS is a small dry-submersible that will take SEALs or other special operatives close to a beach or target area and avoid the fatiguing swim now required there and back (5 or more miles each way). Now, everything can be done underwater, thus maximizing stealth operations in an attack.

The *Greeneville* was capable of 30 knots submerged, and during an emergency main ballast tank blow, the ascent to the surface was fast and nearly blind to the operators. The ascent relies on a series of highly detailed and sequentially planned procedures that allow the submarine to rise in an area where there is no chance of colliding with other shipping or stationary objects, such as buoys.

The *Ehime Maru* was a diesel-powered vessel of 499 gross tonnage/830 tons fully loaded. The *Ehime*

A cradle for the Ehime Maru

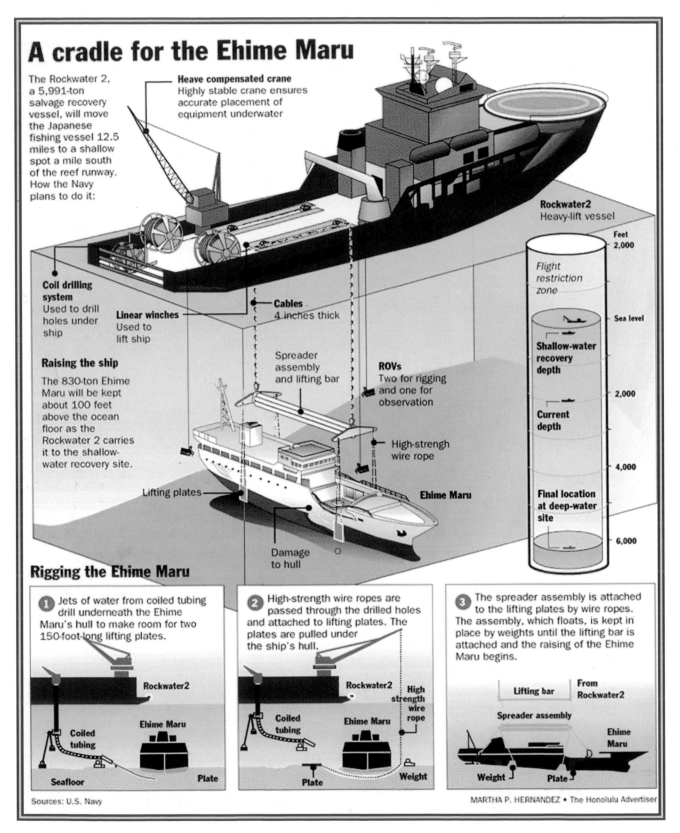

The Rockwater 2, a 5,991-ton salvage recovery vessel, will move the Japanese fishing vessel 12.5 miles to a shallow spot a mile south of the reef runway. How the Navy plans to do it:

Heave compensated crane
Highly stable crane ensures accurate placement of equipment underwater

Rockwater2
Heavy-lift vessel

Coil drilling system
Used to drill holes under ship

Linear winches
Used to lift ship

Cables
4 inches thick

Spreader assembly and lifting bar

ROVs
Two for rigging and one for observation

Raising the ship

The 830-ton Ehime Maru will be kept about 100 feet above the ocean floor as the Rockwater 2 carries it to the shallow-water recovery site.

High-strengh wire rope

Lifting plates

Ehime Maru

Damage to hull

Feet
2,000

Flight restriction zone

Sea level

Shallow-water recovery depth

2,000

Current depth

4,000

Final location at deep-water site

6,000

Rigging the Ehime Maru

1 Jets of water from coiled tubing drill underneath the Ehime Maru's hull to make room for two 150-foot-long lifting plates.

Rockwater2
Ehime Maru
Coiled tubing
Seafloor
Plate

2 High-strength wire ropes are passed through the drilled holes and attached to lifting plates. The plates are pulled under the ship's hull.

Rockwater2
High strength wire rope
Coiled tubing
Ehime Maru
Plate
Weight

3 The spreader assembly is attached to the lifting plates by wire ropes. The assembly, which floats, is kept in place by weights until the lifting bar is attached and the raising of the Ehime Maru begins.

Lifting bar
From Rockwater2
Spreader assembly
Ehime Maru
Weight
Plate

Sources: U.S. Navy

MARTHA P. HERNANDEZ • The Honolulu Advertiser

A block diagram of how the M/V *Rockwater 2* connected to the M/V *Ehime Maru* to bring the sunken school ship to its temporary resting point in the shallow water off the Honolulu International Airport. This was the deepest recovery of a vessel in history. *U.S. Navy*

The M/V *Rockwater 2* with the M/V *Ehime Maru* suspended by an ingenious cradle. In the background, the USNS *Sumner* (T-AGS 61) leads the way. *U.S. Navy*

Maru is one of many Japanese fishing vessels that visit the Hawaiian Islands to instruct young people in the art of fishing.

There are 47 maritime schools in Japan, which is primarily a maritime nation. Thirty-three of these schools offer long-distance excursions to exotic areas for marine life studies and fishing. Fish is a staple of the Japanese diet, and it behooves its society to train young people in the art, culture, and profession of fishing.

The Uwajima Fishery High School makes about three trips to the Hawaiian Islands per year, and there are at least 20 of their boats in the area from Japan at any one time. The trips last about two months each. The Uwajima Fishery High School is located in Uwajima on the Island of Shikoku, about 420 miles from Tokyo.

The *Ehime Maru* and others like it are reasonably modern and seaworthy. They are equipped with up-to-date electronics, and the live-aboard conditions are better than average. However, they are not capable of floating after being struck mortally in their single hull.

The Collision

The submarine *Greeneville* had carried out a number of tests with the Advanced SEAL Delivery System (ASDS) for which it had been modified. After it returned from a port visit to San Francisco in early January 2001, the *Greeneville* was assigned to take 16 guests on a day-long tour at sea. These tours were distinguished visitor (DV) cruises, and this one was slated for seven hours. Several of the guests were involved with the preservation of the USS *Missouri*, which is moored in Pearl Harbor, and others were from Texas.

The *Greeneville* tour involved underwater operations and showed the guests what life was like

UWAJIMA
Fishery-high. school

aboard a nuclear submarine. This tour crowded the boat because it already carried 14 officers and 127 enlisted men. Adding 16 untrained guests overfilled the boat by 11 percent.

Nothing of significance occurred until early afternoon, when a large fishing boat was spotted near the *Greeneville*. However, there was little concern that the vessel would interfere with the submarine's operations. In general, the passengers interfered very little with the operation of the boat. The submarine's commanding officer, Comdr. Scott Waddle, allowed the guests to see as much as physically possible, including being at the controls of the boat when it came to the surface. Untypical as it was, Comdr. Scott Waddle seemed anxious to wind up this expedition so they could make it back to Pearl Harbor at a reasonable time. However, other factors intervened. The weather was poor, and ocean swells were running high. If the Navy hadn't already promised this group a trip on the nuclear-powered vessel, the weather would have prevented the trip.

Those who have been in a nuclear submarine or any submarine will quickly testify as to its tight-fitting quarters. An examination of the submarine after the collision exonerated the guests from causing any harm, other than simply being there and blocking the view of officers and men during critical maneuvers. There was no malice on the guests' part, however, they were crammed into an area where men had gotten accustomed to working with one another and observing screens and terminals from distances without having to ask someone to move. The captain and crew of the *Ehime Maru* were also found free of any wrongdoing. There were no equipment or system failures on either vessel that would have caused or prevented the collision.

In short, the *Ehime Maru* operated in or near the old submarine test and trial area 9 miles off Diamond Head, and the *Greeneville* made preparations to be at a locale known as "Papa Hotel," a point off the entrance to Pearl Harbor. The submarine had planned to be at that point at 2:00 P.M. Unfortunately, for one reason or another, the plan to reach Papa Hotel by the posted plan's time was set back by 30 minutes, and there was a degree of anxiety to make up time. This was a contributing factor in the collision.

U.S. Navy divers swim in and around the M/V *Ehime Maru* to recover items after the ship was transferred to a shallow operating depth. *U.S. Navy*

Navy divers consult with one another on a platform above the M/V *Ehime Maru*. The divers from the Mobile Diving and Salvage Unit One have recovered eight of the nine lost crew from the ship and more than 2,000 personal items. *U.S. Navy*

ensure there is no surface obstruction in the path of the submarine. The submarine requires a large, open space in order to make a correct evolution. Sonar and planned periscope checks that take up to three minutes must be allowed. In this case, only 20 seconds was provided for the required checks. Another difficulty was that the civilians innocently blocked information sources and terminals normally available to the maneuvering crew. The additional passengers onboard stifled feedback and communication among the crew at a crucial moment. The captain announced that he had "a good feel for the contact picture" on the surface and provided some relief to watch standers.

There were at least four contacts on the surface to be considered by the control room of the *Greeneville*. The *Ehime Maru* was given the least attention. The captain of the *Greeneville* decided to accelerate the activities from the deep dive to the ascent to the surface, and thereby assumed most of the command roles himself and bypassed the normal chain of command. He felt confident that the information he had was sufficient for the task at hand, and he proceeded based on partial data. The other three contacts were safely at a 19,000-yard-plus distance, yet, the ignored *Ehime Maru* was within 4,000 yards. There was no indication that the *Ehime Maru* was about to cross the path of the *Greeneville* as it rapidly surfaced, but it did. At 1:43 P.M., the *Greeneville* struck the *Ehime Maru* on its aft port quarter with its hull and heavy-duty rudder. The damage to the *Greeneville* was cosmetic. The damage to the *Ehime Maru* was lethal. The ship sank in 10 minutes and 9 of its 35 occupants were killed. American-Japanese relations in these days were also gravely hurt.

When the submarine maneuvered close to the mark where it would dive to approximately 400 feet in order to demonstrate an emergency main ballast tank surface evolution, civilians were at the controls at some stations. The civilians did not interfere nor contribute to the difficulties that were ahead—it was the fault of the commanding officer. Oddly, the chief of staff to the head of Submarine Pacific was on board, but took no action to intervene, despite his concern over certain obvious anomalies.

The basic plan before making an emergency surface in a non-combat or critical situation is to

The reasons for the collision can be summed into two major categories: There was an inadequate visual and acoustic search of the area where the submarine was about to surface. The other contributing factor was the failure to abide by standing instructions. Information that was vital was not passed on as it

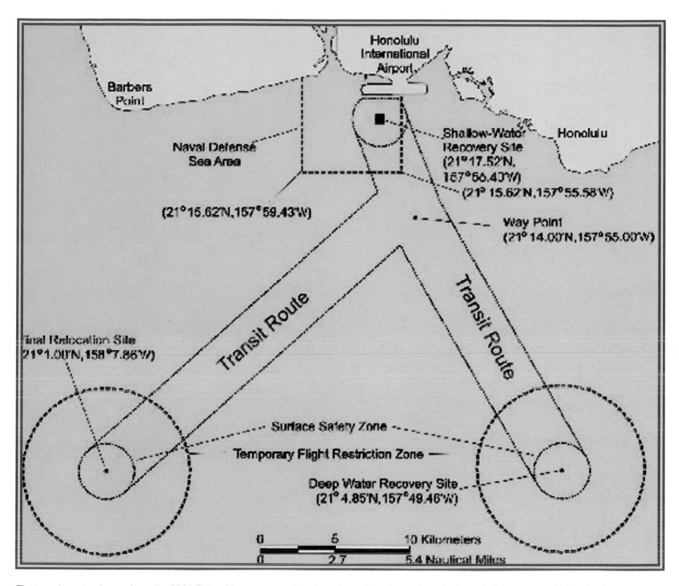

The transit routes from where the M/V *Ehime Maru* was struck and sank to where it was brought into shallow water and then back out to sea, about 12 miles off Barbers Point and approximately 8,500 feet under the surface of the water. *U.S. Navy*

should have been, and the captain created a sense of urgency that caused a sense of complacency among control staff and crew members. Had the captain and his team followed all standing orders and made the proper electronic and periscope sweeps, the procedure to make an emergency ascent probably would have been aborted due to heavy surface traffic.

After the collision, the *Greeneville* searched for survivors, but it could not open its hatches due to high waves. The U.S. Coast Guard and other rescue agencies rescued 26 survivors. The submarine returned to Pearl Harbor to be dry-docked and repaired, its officers and crew under a cloud of suspicion. The *Greeneville*, under new command, later grounded at Saipan and

then collided with the USS *Ogden* (LPD-5) on January 27, 2002, in a third accident.

The *Ehime Maru* slipped under the surface to a depth of more than 1,800 feet and carried nine people with it. It was not an easy decision, but the *Ehime Maru* was brought to a shallow area to salvage personal belongings and search for the nine bodies on the ship. Although it ultimately turned out to be a costly decision for the American taxpayer, it was a show of respect to the Japanese.

Moving the M/V Ehime Maru

On March 4, 2001, a formal U.S. Navy Court of Inquiry was convened, which included a Japanese rear

Final honors are rendered aboard the Japanese submarine rescue vessel Japanese Defense Force (JDF) *Chihaya,* on November 25, 2001. Representatives from three M/V *Ehime Maru* crew members' families threw flowers into the water over the burial site. What began in the conning room of the USS *Greeneville* on February 9, 2001, finally ended on this deck off Barbers Point. *U.S. Navy*

admiral as an adviser. The parties named in the investigation were Comdr. Scott D. Waddle, USN, former commanding officer of the *Greeneville*; Lt. Comdr. Gerald K. Pfeifer, USN, executive officer of the Greeneville; and Lt. Junior Grade Michael J. Coen, USN, officer of the deck (OOD) during the collision.

The Court of Inquiry was established soon after the incident, and a task force was set up with the *Ticonderoga*-class cruiser USS *Port Royal* (CG-73) as the flagship. The USS *Salvor* (ARS-52) and civilian vessels located the wreck of the *Ehime Maru* and brought it to shallow water. Smit-Tak, a Dutch company, was hired as the prime contractor for the job. There were other subcontractors and U.S. and Japanese divers hired to help raise the *Ehime Maru*. Remotely operated vehicles (ROV) were used for the first dives from the *Ocean Hercules*, a 266-foot-long oceanographic cable ship owned by Smit.

A ROV named the *Super Scorpio,* on loan from the U.S. Navy's Deep Submergence Unit in Coronado, California, was deployed soon after the collision and tethered to the commercial vessel M/V *C-Commando*. By February 14, the *Ehime Maru* sat upright about 2,000 feet under the surface. The primary damage was under the ship's hull, apparently where the *Greeneville*'s rudder ripped it open. The hole aft was estimated at 108 square feet. There were other ruptures in the hull from the surfacing of the *Greeneville*, and all contributed to the rapid sinking of the *Ehime Maru*. With the arrival of the M/V *Ocean Hercules*, the remote-controlled *Scorpio III* cut away the masts on the sunken ship and other items that might interfere with the raising of the *Ehime Maru* for transport from 100 feet off the bottom to a shallow area.

On August 1, 2001, the M/V *Rockwater 2* arrived in Honolulu Harbor and prepared for the next phase of what is one of the most expensive salvage jobs in history. The *Rockwater 2* is a state-of-the-art, multi-purpose diving support ship. She was built in 1984 and updated in 1999. The *Rockwater 2* has a helo pad and a dead weight of 5,991 tons. The *Rockwater 2* is also equipped with a 150-ton-weight-/250-ton-lift-capacity crane for offshore and harbor capabilities, and it provides support to all types of divers and diving jobs.

Over the next several months, the activity off Diamond Head moved progressively toward a site selected just off the central part of the main runway of Honolulu International Airport. By early October 2001, the *Ehime Maru* was suspended under the *Rockwater 2* in a cradle built specifically for this particular assignment, and it was slowly taken to its new location. ROVs monitored the entire process from below and relayed real-time data. When the *Ehime Maru* was at its designed depth, authorized divers were deployed to recover bodies and the personal effects of others. A high level of security was maintained to keep unauthorized people out of the area, and those who violated it were given prison time and stiff fines.

Forty-five U.S. Navy divers from the Mobile Diving and Salvage Unit One and eight divers from the Yokosuka Shipyard in Japan made a thorough search of the vessel before they declared it free of human remains.

On November 24, 2001, the *Ehime Maru* began its move to its final location, 12 miles south of Barbers Point at a depth of 8,500 feet.

The Final Voyage

The *Crowley* barge (450-10) lifted the remains of the *Ehime Maru,* and the ocean tug *Sea Valor* towed the barge and remains. The *Ehime Maru* was suspended 90 feet below the barge. Its mast guy wires, fishing nets, and other items had long since been removed. Eight of the nine missing bodies were found.

On November 25, 2001, the *Ehime Maru* was released from the straps holding her to the *Crowley*, and it disappeared into the murky depths of the sea. The total cost was $60 million (U.S.) for this operation. The families of the three Japanese crew members of the *Ehime Maru* gathered aboard the Japanese Self Defense Force submarine rescue vessel *Chihaya* on November 25, 2001, and paid their respects over the location where the ship went down.

The Japanese people were gracious and thanked the people of Hawaii for their efforts and compassion. The time and effort spent by the U.S. government and its people displayed a respect for the Japanese that cannot be underestimated. The former commanding officer of the *Greeneville*, Comdr. Scott Waddle, retired from the U.S. Navy, and traveled to Japan in January 2003 to visit the families of the people lost on the *Ehime Maru*, and pay his final respects.

CHAPTER 3

The old SS *Queen Elizabeth,* or the *Sea Wise University*, burns in Hong Kong Harbor on January 9, 1972, before it sank. This could have been the fate for the M/V *Ecstasy* if the U.S. Coast Guard and other firefighting units hadn't responded to the fire. *TIM*

FIRES AND EXPLOSIONS

M/V Ecstasy (1998)

Carnival Cruise Lines' M/V *Ecstasy* is one of many cruise ships that can be seen in sun ports all over the world. The one thing many of these ships have in common is their boxlike shape. They no longer have the traditional appearance of an ocean liner. The new cruise ships have to carry a large number of passengers, and the object is to have an increasing number of cabins or state rooms with a balcony view. The boxlike shape should not fool the amateur mariner. With full power and stabilizers in use, the *Fascination* class can ride out most heavy seas with ease and comfort. Generally, their courses are laid out by computer, and bridge personnel are present to ensure that all is in working order. A course deviation from that assigned by the computer is allowable for two reasons: imminent danger or to keep the ship in the sunlight. Passengers pay to get a tan, thus, the ship must oblige.

The *Ecstasy* is registered to Panama and is one of the 70,367-ton *Fascination*-class vessels built in Finland by Kvaerner Masa-Yards for the cruise line. She is 855 feet in length, has a 103-foot beam, and can make up to 21 knots on diesel power. The *Ecstasy* can carry up to 2,052 passengers and a crew of 920.

The *Ecstasy* has been at sea for a number of years in the Caribbean and Pacific. She was transferred to the three-day, four-night trips out of San Pedro after she suffered a fire in the aft part of the vessel in 1998. In February 2002, we took a cruise to familiarize ourselves with the firefighting equipment and boat drills. They were excellent, and Carnival Cruise Lines has obviously improved its safety methods.

A Burning Ship Leaves Harbor

On July 20, 1998, the *Ecstasy* was headed from Miami to Key West, Florida. The ship was loaded with 2,565 passengers and 916 crew members (many crew members weren't fluent in English). The ship left just before four in the afternoon and began its trip down the main channel. The main channel is normally filled with the "who's who" of cruise ships, ranging from the most modern to the old and quaint. From 4:54 P.M. until 5:10 P.M., the ship slid down and out of the channel. However, a small fire had been started in the main laundry aft. A welder's spark ignited the fire, and it was forced up through the ventilation system into an area where nylon mooring lines were stored. These are highly flammable, especially under open and forced-air conditions. The heat became intense and produced a lot of smoke.

In the minutes that followed, the passengers and crew knew that something was not right and that they could possibly be in real danger. One newlywed couple filmed the chaos, and when they asked many of the crew for directions, they received petrified stares and no information. Ultimately, it became known that the aft quarter of the vessel was on fire, and passengers should gather forward to avoid smoke, fire, and panic trampling.

One hour after the ship left her mooring, it lost propulsion due to its burned wiring and other issues. People ashore in seaward condominiums quickly dialed 911. The U.S. Coast Guard and six commercial tugboats came to help. The *Ecstasy* drifted north about 8 miles before it was taken under tow at 9:09 P.M., the same time the fire was officially declared out. At 9:30 P.M., the U.S. Coast Guard declared that the *Ecstasy* was safe enough to enter port, and at 1:18 A.M. on July 21, 1998, the ship was tied up at Pier 8 in Miami. Now, the recriminations, examinations, and improvements would begin. Fortunately, no one died during this accident. Fourteen crew members and eight passengers were injured.

An aft photograph of the M/V *Ecstasy* moored in Ensenada, Mexico, in February 2002. The ship, formerly registered under the Liberian flag, now flies the Panamanian flag of national convenience. It was at the lowest of open ports aft when fire was first observed in the laundry area and ventilators. *Author's collection*

The damage to the ship was $17 million, and one passenger had to be hospitalized because of a pre-existing condition.

Why Did This Happen? What if the M/V Ecstasy *Was 500 Miles Out to Sea?*

There are many factors that caused the fire. The ship's welder should never have been working in the laundry. The air ducts were full of lint and carried the fire. There wasn't a fire suppression system on the aft mooring deck and no way to dissipate noxious smoke. The crew was incapable of leading the passengers during the emergency due to language and leadership barriers. They did not seem to know what to do. Herding the passengers away from the lifeboats, their only means of escape, was foolish.

If the fire had occurred at sea, there would have only been a few people to tell the tale. The death toll would have been well over 2,000.

By February 2002, most of the deficiencies noted had been corrected, especially the leadership and language issues. The men and women in charge of giving orders in such a situation are well trained and know to use a loud voice in many languages.

Texas City Disaster (1947)

In the ports that surround Galveston Bay, Texas, there are a number of piers and loading facilities for a variety of cargo. This area is capable of moving 50 or more cargo vessels at once through its port facilities.

On April 16, 1947, there were an estimated 50 cargo vessels of all types loading and unloading goods in Galveston Bay. Several were oil tankers that were loading and unloading petroleum products, many were small vessels for local traffic, and three former *Liberty* ships from World War II were also in port. The former *Liberty* ships played a major part in the Texas City Disaster.

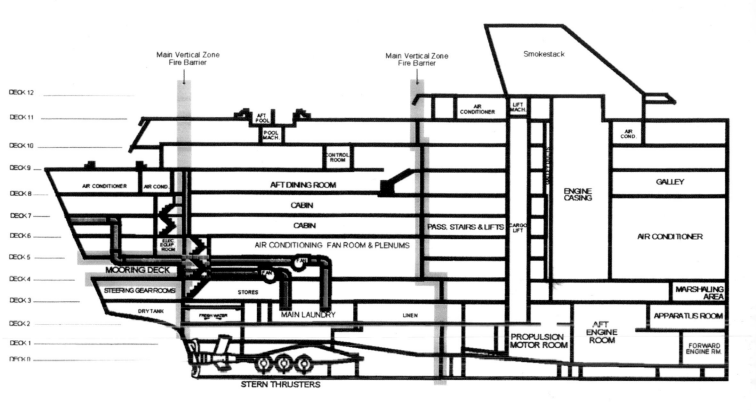

This is the area where the M/V *Ecstasy* burned, as depicted by the National Transportation Safety Board. The main laundry area, just under the mooring deck, is where the fire began, and the ventilating pipes are clearly visible. The fire and smoke moved over one-quarter of the vessel in less than one hour. *National Transportation Safety Board*

All three vessels—the French-registered and French-owned SS *Grandcamp*, the SS *Highflyer*, and the SS *Wilson B. Keene*—were tied to the docking area adjacent to the Monsanto Chemical Company and near four-dozen major oil tanks.

April 16, 1947, dawned with a cool breeze from the north, yet the fumes traditionally associated with an oil-pumping and chemical-storage facility remained. The *Grandcamp* had been sold by the U.S. government to a French company. It was being loaded with ammonium nitrate fertilizer and had been partially filled with cargo. The *Grandcamp* had a good pedigree. She was built in Los Angeles in 1942 and christened the SS *Benjamin R. Curtis*. She was 422.8 feet long, had a beam of 57 feet, and its gross tonnage was 7,176.

There was no overall master plan for dealing with a large-scale disaster such as an explosion or major fire, and conventional wisdom in 1947 was that the region had just come through a major war without any great problems, so any fires and so forth would be dealt with locally. The demilitarized *Grandcamp* was moored at Pier O and, aside from taking on various sundry and other cargo items, was having some work done on her turbine casing. This temporarily immobilized the ship, as the single propeller would not turn over. The *Grandcamp* was going to head back home to Brest, France, and carried bagged shelled peanuts, twine, and some small-arms ammunition in another hold. Fully loaded, the *Grandcamp* carried almost 2,500 tons of ammonium nitrate, among other items.

Ammonium Nitrate: From Explosive to Fertilizer

Ammonium nitrate was manufactured in limited quantities before World War II. Production was vastly increased during the war, because it was a necessary and inexpensive component of explosives, with about half the explosive power of TNT. After the war, the brownish crystalline substance now was in huge surplus, and it served the additional function of being an excellent chemical fertilizer. Texas City alone had shipped over 75,000 tons of

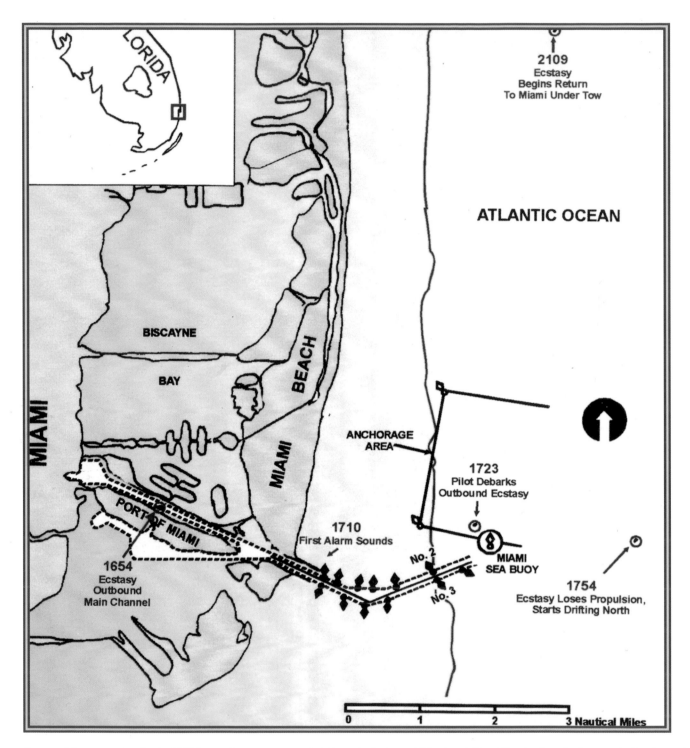

A map of the route taken by the M/V *Ecstasy* from 4:54 P.M. until 9:09 P.M. in the Port of Miami and Miami Beach when the fire was declared out. *National Transportation Safety Board*

A view of the twin exhaust funnels of the M/V *Ecstasy* in February 2002. The passengers were herded to the bow to avoid the fire. *Author's collection*

the material to war-ravaged Europe over the previous two years in ex-*Liberty* ships just like the *Grandcamp* and ex-*Victory* cargo vessels. There were other ports shipping the dangerous material, such as Baltimore, Maryland, and New Orleans, Louisiana. Aside from an abundance of ammonium nitrate, there were surpluses in virtually everything produced for the war effort, including 2,710 *Liberty* ships and thousands of aircraft and other vehicles . The United States had been the arsenal of democracy, and it now was the bargain dealer of the same materials.

The Army Bureau of Ordinance tag on the ammonium nitrate packaging did not alert the civilian handlers to its level of danger. It was handled just like bags of wheat or concrete, as many

later testified, and when the *Grandcamp*'s carpenter, Julien Gueril, smelled smoke from the opened hatch over hold number four, there was no great fear. Safety was quite lax, and despite the prohibitions against smoking cigarettes, it was common for nearly everyone to smoke in all areas except where expressly forbidden. Posted signs were ignored, and some red warning signs had cigarette butts crushed out on them.

Stevedores (men who load and unload the vessels) had started work early that day because there were many vessels to work with, so shortly after 8:00 A.M., they pulled the hatch cover off hold number four and began to work. By 8:25, Gueril and others smelled smoke from the lower level of hold number four, where stacks and stacks of poorly

Passengers prepare for a boat drill before the M/V *Ecstasy* departs. The ship's crew was quite knowledgeable and up to date in lifesaving techniques and took this drill seriously. *Author's collection*

packed ammonium nitrate were stuffed. A fire had begun in the hold, which was nothing new, but it required attention.

The SS Grandcamp *Explodes, Along with Half the Harbor Area*

The crew and some of the stevedores attempted to extinguish the blaze, but it was almost inaccessible because it was located in an area far down in the hold. The smoke took on a yellowish, gold color and obscured the feeble efforts of the men with two small water tanks and the contents of a Thermos jug of ice water. The fire quickly grew beyond the control of a city fire department. A hose was lowered into the hold to spray down the lower areas, but the ship's captain didn't want to damage the cargo and ship with thousands of gallons of water. He convinced all

those around him to cover the hatch, secure it with tarpaulins, and inject steam into the hold to suppress the fire. Hold number five was aft of hold number four, and it contained small-arms ammunition. The ship's captain told the stevedores to unload that hold as a precaution. Unfortunately, the fire grew at a quantum rate, and the suppression technique did not smother the flames. In fact, the steam built up and blew the hatch cover off. The huge plume of smoke attracted several onlookers near the bow of the ship. The events that took place after 9:00 that morning are somewhat debatable, but between 9:12 and 9:15, hold number four in the *Grandcamp* erupted into a fantastic and devastating explosion that all but vaporized the vessel and everyone aboard and around her who were attempting to bring the fire under control. Most of the deaths occurred within 1,000

A frontal view of the M/V *Ecstasy* in the Mexican Port of Ensenada. *Author's collection*

feet of the ship, but the explosion spread throughout the town. One mile away, a chunk of steel from the *Grandcamp* crashed through the roof of an automobile and killed the driver instantly. A small plane above was literally shot out of the sky and the pilot was killed.

The *Grandcamp*, other ships nearby, and the Texas City Terminal Railway Company had sounded their ear-piercing alarms just before the explosion, but they provided little help and warning. The rationale behind the explosion was that the steam, combined with the 880 tons of ammonium nitrate, caused thermal decomposition, and with bunker oil tanks in close proximity, it was only a matter of time before an explosion occurred.

The volunteer fire department had arrived with the Republic Oil firefighting unit, and the explosion killed all of these men. There were a few photos taken before the explosion, but the cameramen left when the flames really got out of control. These are the only record of the *Grandcamp* in its last few minutes as a vessel before being rendered into unrecognizable steel.

The explosion of the *Grandcamp* could be heard more than 150 miles away, and windows were shattered for miles. A mushroom cloud quickly expanded over the center of the explosion to 2,000 feet away, and, within minutes, shrapnel began to fall all over the harbor, the chemical and refining plants, and the neighborhoods close to the harbor. This

The lifeboats on the cruise ship M/V *Ecstasy.* They are fiberglass covered to protect from the elements, have a large passenger capacity, and are powered by diesel engines. The boats have modern electronic sensors to determine location as well as send out distress signals. They are also easy to board and launch. *Author's collection*

caused even greater destruction when other flammable materials fed on the explosion, and minor catastrophes erupted and raged out of control.

The *Grandcamp* and the calamity caused by the ammonium nitrate explosion seemed to be the center for all rescue and firefighting capability. However, another disaster was in the making. The *Highflyer*, owned by the Lykes Brothers, was moored at another slip across from the *Grandcamp*, and the sheer force of the *Grandcamp*'s explosion caused the *Highflyer* to break loose from its moorings and slam into another cargo vessel, the *Wilson B. Keene*. The *Highflyer* was loaded with ammonium nitrate and contained 1,000 tons of sulfur. The *Highflyer* was heavily damaged, yet her crew managed to remain aboard and attempt to keep the fire under control. At 1:10 A.M. on the day following the *Grandcamp*'s explosion, the Texas City

area was rocked with a larger explosion when the *Highflyer* went up like a box of Roman candles. This time, the oily cloud of smoke soared a mile above the harbor area. Tugs had arrived just moments before to pull the smoking and burning ship away from the slip. When it became apparent that it was too late to save the ship, the crews on the tugs tried to rescue what crew and firefighters they could. The *Wilson B. Keene* did not fair much better, as she sank at her mooring. At least parts of her still resembled a ship after the explosions.

The first explosion of the *Grandcamp* destroyed nearly all of Texas City's firefighting equipment and most of its firemen. Further explosions and fires decimated the remaining force plus most of the local emergency personnel. There is no official number of how many were killed in the blasts and in all of the collateral damage, but it is estimated there were 576

The 145-passenger-capacity lifeboats aboard the M/V *Ecstasy* can be easily boarded and launched. A mechanism check revealed that the boats are well serviced and the davits heavily greased. *Author's collection*

TEXAS CITY DISASTER - APRIL 16, 1947
FRENCH VESSEL *S. S. Grand Camp (ex Liberty Ship Benjamin R. Curtis)*
Fire Began in Hold Number 4 (as shown)

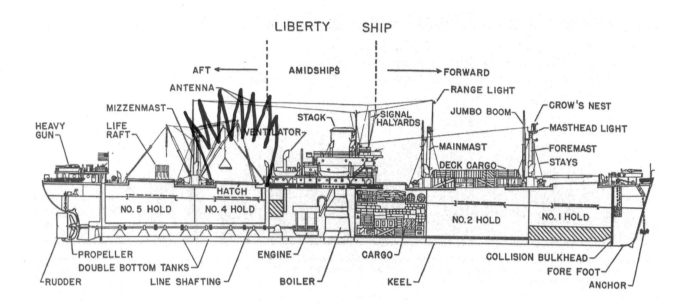

LIBERTY SHIP

AFT ← | AMIDSHIPS | → FORWARD

ANTENNA
MIZZENMAST
HEAVY GUN
LIFE RAFT
VENTILATOR
STACK
SIGNAL HALYARDS
RANGE LIGHT
JUMBO BOOM
CROW'S NEST
MASTHEAD LIGHT
MAINMAST
FOREMAST
STAYS
DECK CARGO

HATCH
NO. 5 HOLD NO. 4 HOLD NO. 2 HOLD NO. I HOLD

PROPELLER
DOUBLE BOTTOM TANKS
RUDDER
LINE SHAFTING
ENGINE
BOILER
CARGO
KEEL
COLLISION BULKHEAD
FORE FOOT
ANCHOR

A cutaway drawing of a *Liberty* ship built during World War II, like the *Grandcamp* and *Highflyer*. Ammonium nitrate was stored in hold number four aboard the SS *Grandcamp*, which is where the fire began. Hold number five held small-arms ammunition. The shell plating was quite thin over the strakes that held the ship together. The *Liberty* ships were the Woolworth cargo ships of World War II and were used to transport materials from the United States to the battlefront. *Liberty* ships were used for decades after the war, although there are only two still officially operable: the SS *Jeremiah O'Brien* in San Francisco, and SS *John W. Brown* on the East Coast. *Author's collection*

The SS *Grandcamp* minutes before it blew up at Pier O at Texas City. Smoke pours from hold number four, and a water hose has been fed up from the dock to the ship. The captain closed the hatch over the hold in an attempt to smother the fire with steam. It did not work. The *Liberty* ship soon exploded with a fury that destroyed everything within several hundred yards, including scores of innocent people. *Disaster Internet Site*

Volunteer firemen and the crew of the SS *Grandcamp* do their best to extinguish the fire now out of control aboard the floating bomb, which was ticking quickly. This was the last known photograph of these brave firemen. *National Archives*

Here are some of the few *Liberty* and *Victory* ships left from World War II at the Suisun Bay Reserve Fleet in July 2002. None are operable, however, in the years following World War II, they could be found under dozens of flags in ports all over the world. There are no longer any trained personnel capable of operating these antique vessels. In the 1940s and early 1950s, they once crowded ports like Texas City. The SS *Wilson B. Keene* was much like the vessels shown rusting away. *Author's collection.*

An aerial view of the chemical and oil refinery area in the Texas City harbor area at the height of the explosions and collateral fires. Tanks full of oil and other flammables also contributed to the explosions as the fires spread. The smoke from this fire could be seen for scores of miles, and shrapnel and burning objects floated down miles away to start other fires. *National Archives*

dead and more than 3,000 injured. Over one-third of Texas City's homes were destroyed or condemned, and the huge Monsanto plant was leveled. Two-thousand people were left homeless. Five-thousand people attended the funeral services for those who were killed. There are many people who were never identified in one of Texas' worst disasters.

Another "It Can't Happen Here" Myth

The U.S. Coast Guard was somewhat unprepared for this magnitude of difficulty, and it could only bring the buoy-tender *Iris* and a small fireboat to assist. In terms of local fire equipment on the water (fireboats), there was very little for the emergency personnel to work with. This was due to the mindset in the immediate postwar years. The thought that "it could not happen here" was pervasive.

Ultimately, 4,000 volunteers assisted in firefighting, first aid, body removal, and cleanup. More than 1,200 medical and aid professionals descended on the area as soon as possible to help. Soon, everything was under control and smoking debris was the only thing left of a $20 million Monsanto plant and a bustling commercial and harbor area. Although the disaster did not occur at sea, ships and their cargo caused the disaster. It pointed out the need for all ports to have a comprehensive plan for preventing catastrophes and reducing their impact should they occur. Comprehensive plans have since been developed for a major emergency.

The remains of a Texas City fire truck after fire and explosions swept over it. A small plane flying overhead was knocked out of the sky during the first blast, and its occupants were incinerated. *National Archives*

A U.S. Coast Guard seagoing buoy-tender was moored in Baltimore Harbor in January 2002. This vessel is identical to the U.S. Coast Guard *Iris* that acted as a firefighting ship during the disaster. Commanded by Lt. Roy Sumrall, the ship was ill-equipped to fight a major conflagration similar to what happened in Texas City, but this did not prevent the *Iris* and the "coasties" from trying. These 935-ton, 180-foot vessels, known as 180-footers, still operate under various civilian and commercial controls. *Author's collection*

The U.S. Coast Guard buoy-tender *Iris* is barely visible at the bottom left. It fought fires alongside the docks in Texas City in April 1947. Another U.S. Coast Guard boat, *C-64309,* plus other small harbor craft, tried to help fight fires, but had no luck. They could not get close enough without endangering the men and boats. *National Archives*

28. "L'ATLANTIQUE"
Paquebot de grand luxe, ligne Sud-Amérique.
Déplacement 40.000 tonnes, Long. 227 m., Larg. 30 m.

This is an advertisement for the SS *L'Atlantique*. The complaints about the bulky, top-heavy look are valid, proven by this photo. The ship lasted three years before it caught on fire. *Author's collection*

SS L'Atlantique (1933)

The SS *L'Atlantique* was built at the Penhoet Shipyards in Saint-Nazaire on the coast of France. The 42,512-ton passenger ship was launched on April 15, 1930, and completed on September 29 of the same year. The main complaint of those who rode the 742-foot long ship and saw her at sea was that she was ugly. Her lines were bulky and sluggish. She appeared top-heavy and lumpy. Taking this into consideration, her owners extended the three smoke funnels upward to make the ship more balanced and aesthetically attractive to the eye. Its stumpy look was not the only drawback to the anticipated profits of the huge ship. A worldwide economic depression witnessed the end of poorly financed shipping lines. Scores of vessels were found nested together in the backwaters of one harbor or another until better days. Shipping lines seem to overbuild ships to take

care of an anticipated huge trade based on history. However, the good times always seem to vanish just as the expensive vessels are being fitted out for service. In reality, many felt that the fire that later destroyed the *L'Atlantique* in 1933 was the result of sabotage in the ship's wiring.

The SS *L'Atlantique* was owned and operated by the Navigation Sud-Atlantique, the same company that owned the famous SS *Ile de France*. The *L'Atlantique* was slated for travel between South America and such ports as Rio De Janeiro, Buenos Aires, Montevideo, Santos, and its home port in Bordeaux, France. The ship was capable of 21 knots on steam turbines connected to four screws, and her passenger complement included 414 in first class, 158 in second class, and 584 in third class.

The interior was built and outfitted in great contrast to the ship's exterior. The *L'Atlantique* was

The burning SS *L'Atlantique* drifts in the English Channel. The smoke was so thick it was impossible to launch boats on the port side, and to do so on the starboard side was difficult at best. The death toll was 19, and if the ship had carried a full complement of passengers, the death toll would have been in the hundreds. *TIM*

A closer look at the water line under funnel number three shows a useless life raft. The smoke is less pronounced at this point in this aerial photograph, and soon, intrepid salvage masters will attempt to board the burning ship to claim it and all that goes with it for salvage. *TIM*

famous for her shopping mall; and the decorations, carpets, and wall designs were on par with any of the best liners at sea.

However, *L'Atlantique* was destroyed by fire. Fortunately, though, the ship had no passengers. She was sailing from Bordeaux to Le Harve to be dry-docked for a hull cleaning and routine overhaul. The commanding officer of the *L'Atlantique* was Capt. Rene Schoofs, and a fire broke out at approximately 3:30 A.M. in an empty first-class stateroom on January 4, 1933. Before the

fire was discovered, it spread through a large number of rooms by following the main electrical wiring. By the time the alarm was raised, it was not possible to save the ship. Wireless pleas for assistance were quickly answered by the SS *Achilles*, SS *Errata*, SS *Ford Castle*, and SS *Ruhr*. Wireless had come a long way since the days of the *Titanic*, but the transmissions from the *L'Atlantique* were short because the operators were overcome by smoke. Just before 6:00 that morning, the order was given to abandon ship. The davit ropes failed and

Tugs compete to get a line on the burned-out hulk of the SS *L'Atlantique*. Dutch, French, and German tugs towed the listing ship into Cherbourg, and all claimed it for salvage. *TIM*

dumped seven men into the icy water of the English Channel. The boiler room crew members stayed at their stations, because they knew it was impossible to leave. They all perished. Incredibly, only 19 died during the fire and rescue effort.

Captain Schoofs leaped from the ship when he ascertained that he was likely the last to leave the ship. He was rescued by a lifeboat from the Dutch steamship *Achilles*. The *Achilles* successfully rescued the balance of the crew that was in the water or

lifeboats. The *L'Atlantique* was ablaze from stem to stern, and smoke poured out of her funnels and ventilators. She was completely burned out. In the late afternoon of January 5, 1933, the ship began to list approximately 20 degrees to port.

A war broke out over who had claim to the red-hot wreckage drifting in the English Channel. Dutch, French, and German tug and salvage masters wanted to lay formal claim to all 40,000 tons of metal floating around before it grounded

The burned out SS *L'Atlantique* in Cherbourg. Many battled for salvage rights, but the ship was ultimately scrapped. *TIM*

somewhere or was ordered sunk by a navy as a hazard to navigation. Two French men risked their life to climb aboard the blackened and smoldering wreck to see that the tricolor French flag floated above the ship. They successfully raised it, but it was soon obliterated by smoke and soot. Ultimately, tugs from all three nations got a line aboard and pulled the drifting liner into Cherbourg. The fire was still burning and the Cherbourg Fire Department eventually put it out on January 8, 1933. The French press even got into the act, saying that the Dutch and Germans had no business claiming salvage of a French ship, despite the bravery of the Dutch when they rescued the crew and officers of the burning ship.

The claims of salvage and insurance were argued in and out of court until February 1936. Finally, Compagnie Sud-Atlantique was awarded $6.8 million, and the burned-out eyesore in Cherbourg was towed to Port Glasgow, where the *L'Atlantique* was reduced to chunks of metal. The *L'Atlantique* was a burned-out wreck for a longer period than she was an ocean liner.

CHAPTER 4

In one of the more spectacular photographs of the sea overcoming a man-made vessel, the 10,000-ton SS *La Jenelle* is pounded by the first of many waves. In 23 minutes, the waves dragged the ship's starboard anchor and chain loose and pushed the *La Jenelle* ashore. Two watchmen were still aboard the ship when this image was taken by photographer Jim Cooluris, who had a photo shop nearby. Minutes later, a coast guard helicopter plucked the terrified watchmen from the wreck, and the ship rolled ashore and onto its port side. *Courtesy Jim Cooluris Photography*

GROUNDINGS, FOUNDERINGS, AND CAPSIZINGS

SS Bahama Star/SS La Jenelle (1970)

For 36 years, the SS *La Jenelle* went through four shipping lines with four previous names. Its most famous was the SS *Bahama Star* from 1960 to 1966. In the end, the 17,114-ton, 466-foot cruise ship was known as the SS *La Jenelle*, a name she carried from 1966 until April 13, 1970. The SS *La Jenelle* had been purchased by the Western Steamship Company, a partner ship of Sorenson and Bayles. The stately but old-fashioned cruise ship had been moved from its traditional sailing territory in the Caribbean to Port Hueneme, California, near Santa Barbara. Before the *La Jenelle* moved to California, it spent its career in the aquamarine waters of the Carribean.

Saving Lives on the SS Yarmouth Castle

The 5,000-ton SS *Yarmouth Castle* was built in 1927 and had a wooden superstructure and plush interior fittings. During an overnight cruise on November 13, 1965, the 38-year-old ship, which had now outgrown its usefulness, had a small fire in unoccupied stateroom 610 that was caused by an improperly stored mattresses that fell onto a lighting system. The fire spread quickly, and without any firefighting tools, the ship was nothing but a floating deathtrap. The fire moved so quickly through the tinder-dry wooden panels of the ship that the captain and his officers had no time to warn passengers of the impending disaster. Safety standards were almost nonexistent, and the only way that the 370 passengers and 175 crew could be saved was to leave the smoldering ship. Some boats were launched with passengers and crew, and others chose the warm waters and hanging onto pieces of wreckage.

The *Bahama Star* made the same run during its three- and four-day cruises to Nassau from Miami each week. It was 40 minutes behind the *Yarmouth Castle*, and the *Bahama Star* sped up when she heard the *Yarmouth Castle*'s cries for help over the radio. It kept with the most sacred of all laws of the sea: save another at all costs. The Finnish M/V *Finnpulp*, was nearby and also turned toward the now-flaming mass aboard the *Yarmouth Castle*. Both rescue ships were soon within range to launch their own boats and pluck people out of the water. Man-eating sharks were in the area, and it became a race against time to get the swimmers in the boats. The *Bahama Star* came so close to the burning ship that its paint blistered and bubbled from the heat while it saved most of those who were rescued. Captain Byron Voutsinas of the *Yarmouth Castle* left his ship in a boat with several of his officers and was seen by the second mate of the *Yarmouth Castle*, Jose Ramos. In a rage, Second Mate Ramos told his cowardly captain to return to his command because there were penalties for what he was doing. Captain Voutsinas continued on his way. He left his responsibility to save his life. Within a few minutes, the ship, now completely burned out, rolled over and sank. The time was 6:05 A.M.

Ninety people lost their life on November 13, 1965, and the rest of the passengers and crew were saved by the *Bahama Star* and the *Finnpulp*. Unfortunately, the heroic efforts of the *Bahama Star* doomed her as a cruise ship, for she was primarily made of wood and had heavy non-fireproof drapes and furniture. It did not take long for the U.S. Congress to use the *Yarmouth Castle*'s disaster to point the finger at any ship built like her, and the *Bahama Star* was in the same category. U.S. Coast Guard safety regulations and the House Subcommittee on Merchant Marine and Fisheries put an end to this fine ship. The international community

A map in a brochure from the original New York & Porto Rico (Puerto Rico) Steamship Company Line before the SS *Borinquen* joined the line in 1930. *Author's collection*

The SS *Yarmouth Castle*, a smaller, 5,000-ton version of the SS *Bahama Star* and other smaller vessels that were in the Caribbean trade as "fun ships." These ships were for people who wanted to drink, meet members of the opposite sex, and gamble. The beauty of its wood superstructure and pilothouse doomed the fun ship to death by fire. *Author's collection*

became involved, and an accord was agreed upon in 1964 that outlawed superstructures built of wood on ships already in existence and forbade construction of any in the future.

The cost to rebuild the *Bahama Star* to comply with new regulations was too high, so the ship was sold to the Western Steamship Company, which consisted of the partnership of Sorenson and Bayles, in 1966.

The SS Bahama Star *Before Its 15 Minutes of Fame*

The *La Jenelle*, before its ignominious end, was a 10,000-net-tonnage cruise ship for the New York and Porto Rico (Puerto Rico) Steamship Company, with a 17,114-ton full load. The ship was driven by two steam turbine engines that turned one screw up to speeds of 21 knots. The ship was 465 feet, 10 inches in length; 59 feet, 10 inches in width; and had

a steel hull with a heavy wood superstructure and interior. It was built at the Bethlehem Steel Company in Quincy, Massachusetts, during the early days of the worldwide economic depression. The ship was characterized by nice accommodations, good food, refrigerated air conditioning, and a huge gaming casino. As soon as the ship left U.S. territorial waters, liquor flowed freely and gambling of every sort was available to people starved for their vices due to prohibition.

The ship was christened the SS *Borinquen* on September 24, 1930, and immediately went to work for the New York & Porto Rico Steamship Co. It made runs from New York to the Caribbean, but her sailing career was primarily confined to the warm waters of the Caribbean with cargo and passengers. From 1930 through 1949, the *Borinquen* made voyage after voyage, except for a short stint as a coastal troop carrier for the United States during World War II.

This is one of the few photos taken of the SS *Yarmouth Castle* inferno by an SS *Bahama Star* passenger. Without the *Bahama Star* and the M/V *Finnpulp*, the majority of the passengers and crew of the *Yarmouth Castle* would have perished due to fire, drowning, the elements, or sharks. This photo is a frame from an 8mm camera, hence the lesser quality. *Author's collection*

In 1949, the ship was sold to the Bull Steamship Company and renamed the SS *Puerto Rico*. Under this moniker and ownership, the 20-year-old ship sailed for five years, when she was sold to the Arosa Lines and renamed the SS *Arosa Star*.

In 1960, the *Arosa Star* was sold to the Eastern Shipping Company and renamed the *Bahama Star*. From 1960 to 1966, the old ship made her way from Miami to Nassau and back twice a week on three- and four-day gambling cruises. There was barely enough time to pull into port to load supplies, and there was almost no time at all to make minor repairs. Unfortunately, this is the downside of making just enough profit to keep a ship moving through the water, the passengers fed, and advertising at a maximum to draw passengers. There is no money or time to make repairs on these old ships, and they progressively become less safe. Eventually, they are too dangerous to go to sea, but they still must go to sea to bring in a profit. It is a catch-22 in the commercial passenger business.

The disrepair finally caught up with the *Bahama Star*, because it traded out of a port in the United States and had to cease operations. It was sold to the

The SS *La Jenelle* was moored at Port Hueneme for the last time in late 1969. The owners, the Western Steamship Company, didn't have funds for moorage costs or any future prospects. *Author's collection*

Western Steamship Company and moved to Port Hueneme in Ventura, California. This time the tattered, rusted old vessel was named the *La Jenelle*. At times, the deteriorating vessel could be found moored in the harbor at Port Hueneme or out in the exposed harbor. Harbor mooring fees were too high for the owners, and they planned to sell the hulk to an Indonesian Company as a floating restaurant or sell it to some other entrepreneur on the West Coast, though this never happened. Finally, the wind, waves, storms, and weather overcame the *La Jenelle*. On April 13, 1970, a gale came up and pounded the helpless vessel as it lay moored with one anchor. The ship, with two watchmen aboard, soon dragged anchor, began to drift ashore, and sunk as it moved. The open port lights and broken windows of the ship allowed thousands of gallons of water to enter, which heeled the ship over on her beam ends with a pronounced port list. The entire shipwreck took less than 23 minutes from the onset of the first waves to the grounding. The two crew men were saved by a U.S. Coast Guard helicopter.

Over the next few days, looters took everything that wasn't nailed down. A serious fire burned out the ship's interior, and a looter was killed in the process. The U.S. Navy owned the entire area and cut off the superstructure of *La Jenelle*. The rest of the ship was filled with rocks and made into a breakwater. Today, fishermen can still see minor parts of the old ship as part of the breakwater, and there is a *La Jenelle* Park in the immediate area.

SS Sea Breeze I *(2000)*

Chief Petty Officer (CPO) Darren Reeves, a rescue swimmer at the Elizabeth City, North Carolina, U.S. Coast Guard Air Base, had never heard of the SS *Sea Breeze I*, but on December 17, 2000, he and the ship spent a memorable hour together. On that day, he and several other air base personnel flew 225 miles to find the sinking ocean liner in its death throes. The only thing standing between life and death for the 34 crew members aboard the ship was the resolute courage of CPO

The stranded SS *La Jenelle* lies on the beach. The U.S. Navy took the hulk in hand and made it into a nice breakwater in the early 1970s. *Author's collection*

Reeves, the other Coast Guard Jayhawk helicopter crews, and the two C-130 Hercules that acted as a command aircraft and flew slow circles around the site in some of the roughest weather on record. CPO Reeves and his crew did the right thing, and the 34 stranded *Sea Breeze I* crew members made it safely back to land. The *Sea Breeze I* sank with little trace and was unobserved by human eyes before another U.S. Coast Guard C-130 could arrive on the scene to verify if the ship was salvageable or a menace to navigation.

SS Sea Breeze I, *a.k.a.* SS Federico C./ SS Royale/SS Starship Royale

The *Sea Breeze I*, like many ships that have survived for over four decades, has had multiple owners, outward appearances, and, of course, different names. The SS *Federico C.* was part of the renowned and respected Costa Lines, and it sailed the world's seas. The *Federico C.* took passengers from Genoa, Italy, to destinations such as Buenos Aires, Argentina, and Sydney, Australia, as a form of immigrant trade. Periodically, the ship stopped at other exotic ports such as Casablanca and Gibraltar, but age and the onset of air travel spelled doom to the ship-bourne passenger industry. The *Federico C.* was not an exception, and by the 1960s, she was under new ownership and on a new sailing route.

Premier Cruises inaugurated its line with a single ship: the *Federico C.*, which was renamed the SS *Royale*. The company was based in Port Canaveral, Florida, and had a direct tie-in with Disney. The rooms were filled to capacity with parents and squealing children as it made short cruises. The trade was catered families that visited Disney's Florida theme parks. Three other aging vessels were added, and the *Royale* was renamed the SS *Starship Royale*, its hull now painted a bright cherry red. Other ships in the Premier family included the SS *Starship Oceanic*, the SS *Starship Atlantic*, and the SS *Starship Majestic*. The ships were located in various locations to take advantage of the trade. The "Starship" prefix, along with the hundreds of gallons of red paint on the hull, had to be added to identify the shipping line. The big red boat concept has been taken over by Disney Cruise Lines with modern-day cruise ships with two and three times the tonnage and amenities of its forebears. Disney Cruises now operate Modern Cruise ships whose passengers recently included President George Bush and his family.

From the port side looking forward, the SS *La Jenelle* looks rather beat up after a storm pushed it ashore. An unused shuffleboard court is on the lower right. *Author's collection*

Ultimately, the *Starship Royale* became too old for its work and was traded to Dolphin Lines and renamed the *Sea Breeze I*. Her hull was painted royal blue, and the ship was refurbished in 1989. At 606 feet in length with full load displacement of 20,416 tons, she could carry 822 passengers. Before Dolphin Cruise Lines embarked on its first cruise, Premier Cruise Lines bought them out and once again owned the ship.

The *Sea Breeze I* had a mixed crew of foreign nationals and was commanded by Greek officers. In the late 1990s, it sailed out of New York on short cruises, and became a gambling ship reminiscent of the 1930s "booze cruises," when young people took cheap cruises beyond the 3-mile U.S. boundaries limit to drink liquor and gamble. Cruises to

Havana, Cuba, and cruises to "nowhere" were very popular. The *Sea Breeze* ultimately did not charge enough for its cruises and was under arrest for nonpayment of debts in Nova Scotia, Canada. Premier had gone bankrupt in 2000, threw everyone out of work, and left 450 passengers stranded aboard a ship "cold iron" (no shore power). The passengers were left to their own devices and had to get their luggage off the ship and onto the dock at Halifax. Watchmen and a skeleton crew kept an eye on the ship.

On December 1, 2000, the ship was sold to New York merchant DJL. Despite an argument in favor to scrap the boat, those who thought the ship had some life left in it prevailed. In mid-December 2000, the ship began its trip to Charleston, South

The hatch cover to the forward cargo hold is open on the SS *La Jenelle*. The fire has already done its work on the superstructure, and the U.S. Navy salvagers will rip off and dispose of the superstructure. The hull was used as the form for a new breakwater that the Navy had needed for years at the entrance to its harbor area. *Author's collection*

Carolina, for repair and overhaul. The captain who had been with the vessel for many years was still in command, and there was a pickup crew from the waterfront in Halifax. The ship was less than 300 miles from land when it encountered a storm off the Virginia Capes.

The engineering plant of the *Sea Breeze I* was cooled by seawater intake, and the feed pump and cooling lines began to leak at a rate greater than the safety system could deal with. The storm broke loose piping that would be adequate under normal circumstances, but the inexperienced crew could not keep up with the engine room flood. The crew surrendered to the fact that the ship was doomed to founder and notified the local U.S. Coast Guard at Elizabeth City, North Carolina, and anyone else who might be close enough to provide assistance.

The Rescue

A call came in at 11:00 A.M. on December 17, 2000, that said an ocean liner had sunk 220 miles offshore. The men and women at the air base were not certain how many people were in danger, but it didn't matter. They were going out to save as many

as possible. It was relatively calm near the base because the storm had just passed by, so the base crew was somewhat fooled by this calm before the storm. The two C-130 Hercules aircraft, also known as "thundering pigs," were closer to the scene and had been in contact with the Greek captain. There were 34 men to rescue, and the ship was poised to founder. It had started to list, and it was now at the mercy of wind and wave.

Two Sikorsky HH-60J Jayhawks with extra fuel tanks were launched from Elizabeth City to the last known position of the *Sea Breeze I*. The Jayhawk has an extended range of 500 miles and carries a crew of four: a pilot, co-pilot, flight mechanic, and rescue swimmer. It can carry a maximum of seven passengers, and has extra room that is vital to administer first aid.

ABC television had equipped the Jayhawk that CPO Reeves, a rescue swimmer, was in with a number of small video cameras, on the chance that the helicopter might be involved in a rescue. It is general practice to carry a hand-held camera in each helicopter to record rescue activity, if possible. In the case of CPO Reeves' Jayhawk, the pilot turned on all

The SS *Sea Breeze I* at a pier in New York Harbor during a Tall Ships Week in 2000. The *Sea Breeze I* is still operational and can be seen at the bottom left of the photograph. The aircraft carrier USS *John F. Kennedy* (CV-67) is in the center of the photograph. The former USS *Intrepid,* now the centerpiece of the Intrepid Sea-Air-Space Museum, is at the top of the photograph. *Author's collection*

of the video units when they arrived over the ship. The biggest surprise was that the ship was still afloat and bobbed around like a cork in 35- to 50-foot waves. The C-130s had informed the Jayhawk pilots of what to expect, yet it was almost incredible to see this 606-foot vessel trapped by a storm in the distance. CPO Reeves confided that he was apprehensive, as were others in the rescue party. When he saw the ship through the frosty window of the bumping helicopter, he knew there was a whole

new series of problems. The winds were more than 70 knots, and the waves were higher than he had ever seen. He knew he would have to jump into frigid water to save people.

Men from the *Sea Breeze I* screamed into the radio to the C-130 that the steering engines were frozen and the flooding was progressing fast. The crew had attempted to launch a raft, but it blew away in the wind. The only chance for survival was via a helicopter.

Fortunately, the tired old ship was pointed into the high winds, so a stern approach by the Jayhawk with CPO Reeves was possible. The helo came in above the aft part of the ship and began to lower CPO Reeves from the helicopter. On the first attempt, he was slammed against the hull. The next attempt brought him to the deck. The C-130 instructed the Greek captain on the *Sea Breeze I* to send out only 17 men for the initial rescue. Unfortunately, as CPO Reeves finally made it to the deck with the rescue basket, there was a mad rush from the terrified crew to get aboard the basket, which was equipped to handle, at most, two people at a time. CPO Reeves had to establish order, and with hand signals and his forceful voice and mannerisms, he commanded the frightened men to line up alongside a railing and then selected those who would be hoisted aloft. He knew that the two helicopters could carry a maximum of 20 people, but he never dreamed what would eventually happen. The men were hoisted 40 to 50 feet to the helicopter. CPO Reeves watched as the first eight crew men were pulled up, and he shivered with the thought that he could be left aboard the ship and his 15 year U.S. Coast Guard career would come to end at the bottom of the sea. As the ship continued to bob out from underneath his feet, he watched with some skepticism as the crew chief kept signaling him to send up two more. Just before the last of an amazing 26 crew men of the *Sea Breeze I* was hoisted up, the remaining group again rushed the basket. CPO Reeves had to push them back and tell them, which was difficult with an international crew, that the second helicopter would pick up the rest of the crew.

At long last, the flight mechanic signaled it was time to extract CPO Reeves and shove off. They were overloaded beyond any manufacturer's suggested load limit, but CPO Reeves tried to make the case that he should stay to help the next helicopter. The pilot of the Jayhawk would not hear of it and told him to come up and squeeze in. CPO Reeves came up to what was a human mass much like a clown car at the circus. He got in, the door was shut, and the Jayhawk began its two-and-a-half-hour trip back to Elizabeth City.

The SS *Sea Breeze I* has a new coat of paint shorn of the Disney-red boat trappings. This is how the old ship looked before it deteriorated and rusted. Her new owners thought they might get a few more years out of her, but the elements and age were against their plans. On December 17, 2000, the 42-year-old liner foundered 230 miles off North Carolina. *Steamboat Bill*

The C-130 Hercules is one of the most popular aircraft in U.S. government service. It is also the long-range search and rescue craft for the U.S. Coast Guard, which has a fleet of 27, with 22 in operation. The C-130 Hercules has four Allison T-56 engines and up to a 4,400-nautical-mile range, depending on the mission. It cruises at 280 knots and can carry rescue equipment and rafts. Its crews continuously practice their drops and can hit a rescue site with great accuracy with needed equipment and supplies. Two C-130s worked in tandem with Jayhawk rescue helicopters over the SS *Sea Breeze I*. The command pilot in the C-130 worked directly with the captain of the sinking ship to coordinate the rescue. *Author's collection*

It became so hot, humid, and stuffy in the helo that a window had to be opened. The only way to open the window was for two men to use another man's arm and hand as a wrench to turn the crank to open the window. With an open window for the last hour of the trip, conditions were better, and the people weren't as sullen. No one got sick, which was amazing considering the buffeting the aircraft took during the trip. The same could not be said for the C-130 crew. They used up all of the air sickness bags aboard their aircraft.

The second Jayhawk rescued eight men from the stricken liner after CPO Reeves and his stuffed helicopter left for home, and by mid-afternoon all of the 34 crew members were on solid ground. The U.S. Coast Guard had done what it was supposed to do, and CPO Reeves and his crew demonstrated a tremendous amount of courage. For his efforts, CPO Reeves was awarded one of the U.S. Coast Guard's highest honors, but his real reward was the knowledge that he was instrumental in the rescue of 34 men. During a later search, the only thing left of

the *Sea Breeze I* was an empty lifeboat and some debris. Thirty-four men would have died if it hadn't been for the U.S. Coast Guard.

Tanker Jessica (2001)

In the late evening of January 16, 2001, an 835-ton tanker named *Jessica*, owned by Acotramar, ran aground in the Galapagos Islands. The 28-year-old *Jessica* was on its way into a harbor near San Cristobal Island in Wreck Bay to deliver fuel oil to warships participating in a naval exercise and to the local ecotourism vessel, the M/V *Galapagos Explorer*. The *Jessica* had rarely been to the region, and although it was certified for operations by most governments, it would not pass safety regulations in American harbors. The *Jessica* did not have a double bottom, was old, and its navigational equipment and charts were out of date.

Capt. Tarquino Arevalo, the Ecuadorian tanker's commanding officer, quickly assumed the blame for the accident and stated that the pilot and he were at fault while they steered the vessel into the anchorage.

An HH-60 Jayhawk, the medium-range search and rescue asset of the U.S. Coast Guard, lifts off at the San Diego Coast Guard Air Base in October 2002. It has a 300-mile range and a 45-minute loiter time over a rescue site under most normal circumstances. *Author's collection*

They mistook a signal buoy for a lighthouse, the pounding surf was a distraction, and without updated charts, the ship ran aground. Unfortunately, the harbor's bottom was rocky, and the single-hulled vessel was pried open like a tin can. Oil immediately poured out as the *Jessica* heeled over to starboard, a half-mile from a safe mooring at San Cristobal. The ship sustained minimal damage in the engine room, but to a mariner's eye, the ship was doomed. It was hung up on a craggy rock formation that tore its rust-encrusted, heavily pitted hull apart, and the cargo spilled out into the harbor.

The *Jessica* carried a load of 600 tons (160,000 gallons) of diesel oil for Baltra Island's fuel-storage dispatch station, and 300 tons (80,000 gallons) of intermediate fuel oil (IFO) for the *Galapagos Explorer*. IFO is also known as bunker C fuel, and despite the

A Jayhawk hovers over a field in San Diego. This is what the crew of the SS *Sea Breeze I* saw when CPO Darren Reeves' aircraft came over the stern of the pitching and rolling vessel. *Author's collection*

CPO Darren Reeves' Jayhawk comes in over the stern of the out-of-control SS *Sea Breeze I* in the midst of a major storm off North Carolina on December 17, 2000. *U.S. Coast Guard*

vehement protests by the Galapagos Park authorities, the company that owns and operates the *Galapagos Explorer* was granted a license to operate by the cash-strapped Ecuadorian government. In addition to its cargo of fuel, the *Jessica* carried 6,000 gallons of diesel fuel for its own engine.

The *Galapagos Explorer* had gone to the fuel depot at Baltra Island for its allotment of fuel, but due to scheduling problems, allowances were made for the tourist ship to meet the *Jessica* at San Cristobal. This was something out of the ordinary, considering the captain of the *Jessica* had no chart of the harbor and his vessel was mechanically and electronically unfit for service as a tanker, let alone equipped for a refueling station at sea.

There wasn't a serious oil spill until January 20, 2001, when one of the IFO tanks began to leak. Local fishermen, volunteers, and naval personnel immediately attempted to contain the IFO and reduce the effects of the spill on local flora and fauna. This was particularly important because of the locale of the spill and the impact on international scientific research.

Unfortunately, the *Jessica* was not insured for environmental contamination. The tanker only carried 300 tons of fuel oil, and insurance is required only for vessels carrying 2,000 or more tons. The cost for cleanup and containment would have to come from another pocket.

The Galapagos Islands

The Galapagos Islands became internationally famous after a visit by Charles Darwin and the publication of his revolutionary approach to life, *Origin of Species by Means of Natural Selection.* Darwin sailed through the islands, which are some 600 miles off the coast of Ecuador, aboard the HMS *Beagle* in 1835 during a worldwide voyage that lasted

A mock search and rescue where a rescue swimmer is lowered into San Diego Bay to simulate what it was like when CPO Darren Reeves was lowered onto the SS *Sea Breeze I.* When he was first lowered, CPO Reeves nearly went into the sea, but the Jayhawk crew brought him up on deck. Aside from keeping an eye on the rescue swimmer and the people being saved, the pilots must ensure that the aircraft doesn't crash. *Author's collection*

The cramped cockpit of the Jayhawk. *Author's collection*

from 1831 through 1836. The islands total 2,868 square miles located on the equator and are part of an archipelago. Sixty of the islands are named, and the major ones are Freudian, Baltra, Isabela, Santa Cruz, and San Cristobal. Ecuador declared approximately 97 percent of the total land area as a national park in 1959, and the islands are patrolled by its navy. It maintains a naval facility in the Galapagos Archipelago and does not take oil spills or any other offenses against nature lightly. In the case of the captain and 13 crew members of the *Jessica*, all were confined under arrest at a military facility at San Cristobal. The Galapagos is one of the most volcanically active areas in the world, and much of its land surface is

dominated by black, craggy volcanic rocks. The region has also been designated as a World Heritage Site, and the surrounding waters are a marine nature reserve under the protection of special laws passed by Ecuador.

What sets the Galapagos Archipelago apart from every other location in the world is that it is home to more than 5,000 separate species, and 1,900 of those species do not exist on any other part of the planet. The species exist in the sea and on land. Most depend on the sea for one thing or another, as do nearly 1,000 fishermen who provide legal fish for the 16,000-person population of the island and for many others on the mainland. The government has issued over 50,000 permanent-resident cards, which means that several thousand people live on the mainland and periodically come to Galapagos and fish. The $250 permanent-resident permit also serves as a quasi-surrogate fishing license. For a government that needs money, financial need clashes with the moral obligation to nature. In a sense, the whole issue surrounding the loss of the *Jessica* is one of financial expediency versus obligation to nature. Nature lost on January 16, 2001, but it is making a comeback.

Many of the species on the island are under intense study by scientists, and any destruction or contamination of the environment or ecosystem is equal to the destruction of the great pyramids and other historical one-of-a-kind artifacts. The study of certain species in the Galapagos gives the world a look into the past and what the planet once looked like far before man invented the wheel.

Immediate concern after the *Jessica*'s grounding centered on marine life that was being contaminated by slow leaks from the vessel. Seventeen rare sea birds and seven sea lions were affected and required aggressive treatment. By January 20, it was apparent that local resources, including approximately 200 volunteers, could not prevent 900-plus tons from leaking out of the ship. The *Jessica* was buffeted by heavy surf, and her 28-year-old hull was split open and allowed oil to leak. Help from another source was clearly needed or the spill would do irreparable damage.

The survivor compartment, complete with rescue basket and first-aid kit. In the case of the SS *Sea Breeze I* rescue, there were 28 people crammed in this and the area forward, including CPO Darren Reeves and the flight mechanic. No one was sick, but it was awfully foul in there for the two-and-a-half-hour flight home. No matter, they were alive and somewhat well. *Author's collection*

As a ship ages, its deck and hull begins to rust. Most rust areas are just covered with multiple layers of paint, but after the years take their toll, holes begin to appear. This is probably what the SS *Sea Breeze I* looked like under the waterline. This photo of is an inter-island ferry in the Mediterranean. *Author's collection*

Men pile out of the Jayhawk like a circus-clown car, but there aren't smiles on their faces. They were safe, but what an ordeal. This is likely one of the greatest rescues in maritime history. *U.S. Coast Guard*

View of the tanker *Jessica* shortly after its grounding. The oil spill is now evident, and some containment measures have been initiated. The twice-daily flights over the scene kept authorities in the know about the extent of the spill and what resources were needed and where. *U.S. Coast Guard*

A U.S. Coast Guard C-130 Hercules search and rescue aircraft from Mobile, Alabama, brought in specialized supplies and equipment to assist in the containment and cleanup of the tanker *Jessica*'s spill. The aircraft sits on the ground at an airfield in the Galapagos Islands. Some of the advantages provided by the United States included the expertise of the National Strike Force and pumps designed for extracting oil from vessels that encounter difficulties similar to the tanker *Jessica* and the M/V *New Carissa*'s grounding off of Coos Bay, Oregon. *U.S. Coast Guard*

The badly damaged tanker *Jessica* heeled over and resting precariously on the outcropping of rocks below. The water around the vessel is deep, indicated by its color in the photos. The ship came to rest within 800 meters of the intended refuge its captain sought off San Cristobal Island. Two U.S. Coast Guard petty officers who are members of the National Strike Force from the United States stand by and look over the scene on the port side up forward. Rust and oil are everywhere, as can be seen in this view of the ship. *U.S. Coast Guard*

Containment and Cleanup

Twice-daily flights over the wreckage indicated where the slick was moving, the degree of the leaks from the *Jessica*, and if the oil was sinking to the bottom in any area. This was particularly important because algae that is common to the archipelago is vital in the food chain to sustain animal life, including some of the rare species.

By January 20, the slick covered 1,000 square kilometers, drifted around a number of islands, and hit the beaches. The slick's movement was ably assisted by the wind and the wave/current patterns in the region. The government of Ecuador requested assistance from the international community, including the United States. Within hours, the U.S. Coast Guard was on the scene, and on January 22, the barge *Cirius* was tied up alongside the stricken

ship and pumped oil from the *Jessica*. A team from the Coast Guard National Strike Force, including staff from the National Oceanic and Atmospheric Administration, flew to the Galapagos with high-capacity oil pumps specially designed for offloading oil from ships in trouble. The United States has experienced some rather bad oil spills, such as the *Exxon Valdez*, and has formally designated strike forces in regions along U.S. coastlines to respond to oil spills and contain them before they get out of hand. This particular strike force left its base in Mobile, Alabama (NSF Gulf Strike Team), and went to the Galapagos to assist.

Work continued on the port side of the *Jessica*, and her fuel tanks were successfully loaded onto the *Cirius*. In order to remove the oil from the starboard tanks, the ship had to be brought up on an even keel.

An aerial view shows the barge *Cirius* taking on oil from the tanker *Jessica*. It pumped out water at the same time. A cluster of other boats with volunteers stands by to help. There was never a shortage of volunteers who wished to be part of the cleanup. *U.S. Coast Guard*

All attempts at this failed. By that time, it was decided that any efforts to right the vessel would end in failure. The amount of remaining oil was less than 1,000 gallons, and sorbent would be employed on this elusive mess. More help was on the way from private companies in the United States that specialized in oil spill recovery and cleanup.

On January 31, 2001, the U.S. Coast Guard loaded a C-130 Hercules Search and Rescue (SAR) aircraft with supplies donated by companies in the United States to help resolve the oil spill situation in the Galapagos. Tosco Refining Company of New Jersey donated bales of oil-snare rope, sorbent booms, sorbent pads, and other materials to clean up the spill. Clean Harbors Cooperative of New Jersey donated 100 feet of oil spill containment boom plus anchors and buoys for the boom.

Despite the heroic efforts of hundreds of volunteers, the strike force from the United States, and donations from private firms, the spill was still quite bad. It totaled approximately 250 tons (250,000 gallons) of diesel and IFO fuel and contaminated 1,300 miles of coastline. The efforts of the volunteers, merchant mariners, park rangers, and others collected

approximately 4,200 gallons around the stranded ship using booms, sorbent, and other oil spill equipment. The rest of the fuel oil and diesel (600 tons) was removed by the U.S. Coast Guard and Ecuadorian Naval Forces and transferred to the *Cirius*.

By the end of January 2001, the oil spill from the tanker *Jessica* was under control and left to local resources. Ultimately, the remaining oil film on the water drifted out to sea and was carried away from the fragile islands by slow-moving currents. The fatalities included sea birds and some of the beaches. As for the *Jessica*, often no decision is the best decision. The rusting and rotting hulk has begun its return to nature. This has been hastened by wind and wave, and it is gradually disappearing under the sea. By 2004, the ship should be part of an excellent form of biodiversity.

The small vessel M/V *Multiplex Brisk* riding high (empty and seeking cargo) as it makes its way up a tributary of the Mississippi River within 5 miles of downtown New Orleans, Louisiana, in June 2001. The ship may look boxy, but it is a lot like the tanker *Jessica,* except the *Multiplex Brisk* has a double-bottom, updated and working pumps, state-of-the-art electronics, safety equipment, and adequate charts. *Author's collection*

CHAPTER 5

An aft-quarter view of the SS *Zam Zam* shows the Egyptian flag and no armaments. Her home port was Alexandria. The sign on the railing is in Arabic and English and warns other vessels and small boats that the ship is a twin-screw vessel and to stand clear. *San Francisco Call Bulletin (SFCB)–TIM*

UNEXPLAINED AND MYSTERIOUS OCCURRENCES

SS Zam Zam (1941)

The SS *Zam Zam* was one of thousands of tramp steamers that plied the world's sea lanes and carried cargo and passengers. At 447 feet in length with a 54-foot beam, the 8,300-ton World War I veteran was built in 1909 and employed triple expansion engines that drove two screws and could make up to 14 knots in a following sea and no wind. The big advantage was that the ship was available for travel into an increasingly dangerous war zone. She flew the Egyptian flag and was manned by 120 Egyptian seaman, hotel staff, and officers, except for a few British officers, including Capt. William Gray Smith, who had 37 years of experience at sea, several aboard the *Zam Zam*. Her age was further belied by the fact she had four raked masts, an attractive bow flare, and a high-curved transom. Overall, the *Zam Zam* was an attractive but aging vessel. The ship also carried a working wireless and a well-stocked bar. The latter seemed more important than the former to several of the passengers. She was an old *Bibby* liner, and by this time in her career, was the pride of the Egyptian passenger/cargo fleet. Unfortunately, the fact that the *Zam Zam* was once a *Bibby* liner made her suspect as a British auxiliary training vessel or transport. Neither was true, but the German sea raider *Number 16*, or the infamous *Atlantis*, attacked the unarmed *Zam Zam* on the morning of April 17, 1941.

The old ship began her career as the SS *Leicestershire*. After five years of commercial service, she was pressed into the war effort, and the trusty cargo/passenger combination ship was rebuilt to accommodate hundreds of seasick doughboys of the U.S. American Expeditionary Force under General John Joseph "Blackjack" Pershing. The trip was from New York or any other suitable port on the East Coast to France or England. Imagine rolling on a tub like this for days on end with your destination the trenches of war. The war ended in November 1918, and for many of those same soldiers that made the trip over on the SS *Leicestershire*, the return meant sailing back on the same old tub.

The *Leicestershire* was rebuilt and all of the extra bunks and vestiges of war were removed. By 1919, the ship was back on its normal run from Great Britain to Burma and back. She was renamed the SS *British Explorer* and roamed East Asian ports for the next 14 years, taking whatever cargo or passengers it could sign on for any kind of profit. The quality of its crew and officers was reflected in the variety of cargo and people the ship carried. The ship was a pure tramp steamer.

A Rare Floating Mosque

In 1933, the beat-up old steamer was sold to Egyptian interests represented by the Societe Mier de Navigation Maritime and was homeported out of Alexandria. The ship was cleaned up and refitted to carry pilgrims from Suez to the Port of Jeddah (Mecca). A mosque was built in one of its holds for the religious pilgrims, and the ship was renamed *Zam Zam* in honor of a sacred Mohammedan well near Mecca. From 1933 to 1941, the ship routinely took up to 600 pilgrims on their religious voyages and was likely one of the few floating mosques on maritime record. By early 1941, the war in the Mediterranean was in such a fury that it was too dangerous to make the pilgrimages, even for the religious zealots, so the trips were stopped until the war moved to another region of the world.

The *Zam Zam* was placed back in general trade in the backwaters of New York Harbor. She had just made a trip from the Middle East with a

A rare photo of the SS *Zam Zam* in the port of New York after its trip back from the war zone in early 1941. A closer inspection shows bomb-fragment damage from the near misses of bombs dropped by Italian bombers in Alexandria Harbor in the Mediterranean. *SFCB–TIM*

cargo of high-grade cotton and other miscellaneous items and was awaiting cargo and passengers going to South America, South Africa, and back to the Mediterranean.

Cargo was easily found, because agents were anxious to transport American products to the war zones. They could secure a premium for anything sold in these areas, but it was difficult to find a ship to carry them through waters now infested with U-boats and surface raiders. The cargo had to be non-military, so trucks, automobiles, and farm implements were loaded along with a motley group of passengers who should never have been cooped up on a 447-foot ship.

One hundred Catholic and Protestant missionaries purchased tickets to Africa to convert heathen people. The rest of the passengers included the missionaries' children; a group of young wives of Royal Air Force men on their way to meet their husbands in North Africa; a group of hard-drinking, experienced businessmen; David E. Scherman, a noted *LIFE* magazine photographer; and 24 prospective ambulance drivers who wanted to join the Free French Forces. The 24 young men had been chosen from among 700 of the finest and most exclusive Eastern families and were considered the best of the best.

The ship dropped its mooring lines on March 20, 1941, on its first leg to Recife, Brazil. Although the weather was pleasant, the dynamics aboard the ship had divided the passengers into various camps. The ambulance drivers complained about the high price of the drinks, but after they drank a couple, they did not seem to care. They also teased the missionaries, whom they openly called "bible thumpers" and "sky pilots." The missionaries were determined to prepare themselves spiritually for their new work, so they intensified an attitude of Christian reverence and solitude aboard ship. This instigated the ambulance drivers' pranks. By the time the ship reached Recife, a truce had somewhat been negotiated amongst the passengers, which consisted of 73 women, 35 children, and 94 men. In terms of nationality, there were 138 Americans, 26 Canadians, 25 British, 5 South Africans, 4 Belgians, an Italian, a Norwegian, and 2 people with Greek passports. The 128-member crew was primarily Egyptian and acted as stewards and served the passengers.

On April 8, 1941, the ship plodded onward from Recife toward Cape Town, South Africa. Another ship, an armed pirate of the seas bearing the swastika, was also at sea and hunting for prey. Between the surface raiders and U-boats, the Allies had been forced to sail in convoys and abandon certain sea lanes that lacked heavy concentrations of warships to protect commerce. This meant cruisers fought surface raiders, whether they were Nazi auxiliary cruisers or heavily armed conventional German warships. For this reason, raiders like the *Atlantis* could range far and wide. However, it was important that the communications systems of their targets could be knocked out before a distress message could be sent. This meant the enemy ship was shelled instead of the more chivalrous past practice of placing a shell over the bow and instructing the target vessel to not signal they were being attacked by a raider. Allied shipping no longer stood aside, and as soon as danger approached, they sent a distress signal and their position. Capt. Bernhard Rogge, the commanding officer of the *Atlantis*, soon had to hit his intended victim to prevent a wireless signal.

The *Zam Zam* headed toward South Africa without any escort, as she was not considered a valuable war asset. The proximity of the ship to the equator and the lack of any breeze and air conditioning onboard made sleeping within the ship almost unbearable. Many attempted to sleep topside, but they were interrupted by periodic rain showers or crew men hosing down the decks at 5:30 A.M. The spirit of adventure and wanderlust quickly unraveled, and life became more and more miserable. The only relief was the adequate supply of liquor in the small bar. On April 17 at 6:00 A.M., another ship, whose intentions were not pleasant, was sighted. The *Zam Zam* had run up against the famous German sea raider *Number 16*, also known as the *Atlantis*.

Raider Number 16: The German Armed Merchant Cruiser (AMC) Atlantis

The *Atlantis* was a converted Hansa liner that was named the M/V *Goldenfels*. The ship displaced 7,862 tons and was known as *Raider 16* to the German Navy, the *Atlantis* to its crew, and the *Raider C* to the British Royal Navy. The *Atlantis* was 500 feet in length with a 60-foot beam and drew 25 feet. Her powerplant drove the ship at a maximum of 17.5 knots. Before the war, the *Goldenfels* was strengthened to accommodate certain armaments in time of war. Consequently, it only took 14 weeks for the ship to be prepared for merchant raiding. The *Atlantis* was armed with six 150-millimeter (5.9-inch) guns, a 75-millimeter bow gun, twin 37-millimeter anti-aircraft guns, and four 20-millimeter close-in weapons systems. Aside from these conventional weapons, the ship carried two HE-114 scout seaplanes, amidships (waterline sited)

The infamous bar area aboard the SS *Zam Zam* where businessmen, Royal Air Force pilots' wives, and the cadre of irrepressible ambulance drivers spent much of their time during the voyage. There, they drank overpriced drinks, including a potent concoction called the ZamZam. The missionaries frowned upon the bar and its inhabitants, and, on more than one occasion, attempted to get the captain to close it down. It was too profitable for that, however. *TIM*

torpedo tubes, and had the ability to sew up to 92 magnetic mines. The crew consisted of 328 skilled ratings and 21 of the best German naval officers. The *Atlantis* was commissioned on December 19, 1939. The new raider was shortly put to sea, avoided the British patrols, and searched the world's oceans for merchant men whose cargo had to be destroyed. Of course, some of the cargo found its way onto the deck of the *Atlantis* and the six other major armed merchant raiders that were at sea.

The *Atlantis* changed its appearance on numerous occasions to fool its prey and those that might actively hunt the wily warship. The *Atlantis* was the most successful of all the German raiders. It cruised more than 102,000 nautical miles over 622 days and destroyed 22 vessels for an aggregate total of 145,697 tons of Allied shipping. Overall, the seven armed merchant raiders in the German program netted 87 ships for a total of over 600,000 tons of cargo

destroyed. These were heavily armed vessels that required a light cruiser with 6-inch guns to run them aground, and there was always a lurking U-boat in the vicinity to contend with should the raider be destroyed. Ships like the *Atlantis* also carried out a collateral mission to hunt and tie up Allied warships and embarrass the British Royal Navy.

The SS Zam Zam *and the* (AMC) Atlantis *Meet*

The *Atlantis* had been at sea for many months and had a very successful cruise when it began stalking the *Zam Zam* just after midnight on April 17, 1941. Both vessels were about midway between South America and Africa when the *Zam Zam*'s radio operator began to hear cries of help from the Norwegian freighter SS *Blue Star*. The call for help was about a German surface raider shelling their vessel, and then the radio signal faded out.

Opposite: A photo of the *Zam Zam* entering New York Harbor in February 1941. Her owners sought cargo and passengers for a voyage to Recife, Cape Town, South Africa, and back to Alexandria. The vessel waited a few weeks to fill her holds and cabins, and left on what was her last journey. *SFCB-TIM*

The day before this call for help, a *Blue Star* life preserver had been seen floating in some wreckage. Nothing more was thought of the incident, yet at about 6:00 A.M., a ship came over the horizon. It appeared to be the Norwegian freighter SS *Tamesis*, but looks can be deceiving, especially when a series of 5.9-inch and 75-millimeter shells hit your ship with deadly accuracy. Captain Rogge of the *Atlantis* assumed the *Zam Zam* was a British armed merchant cruiser and took no chances. He wanted to sink the ship before she could respond. The Egyptian flags painted on the superstructure and steaming ensign were not recognizable to the *Atlantis* in the predawn light.

The crew of the *Zam Zam* began to jump over the side of the ship into the warm waters of the South Atlantic, and other crew members and passengers rushed to the lifeboats. Not everyone decided to leave the dubious comfort and safety of the *Zam Zam* so quickly. There were a few regulars in the bar who refused to give up their seats, and a couple of missionaries screamed that it was the wrath of God brought down on the sinners. Finally, all were convinced to leave.

Over on the *Atlantis*, Captain Rogge realized he had made one of the biggest mistakes of his professional life. He had fired upon a neutral vessel and now had to deal with some 300 neutral but, very likely, belligerent people. Fortunately, no one was killed during the unprovoked attack, yet, it was necessary to dispatch the old liner with demolitions. As the boats left the *Zam Zam* for the *Atlantis*, German demoli-

Boats pull away from the SS *Zam Zam* after it had been hit nine times by the *Atlantis* with its 150- and 75-millimeter guns on April 17, 1941. The *Zam Zam* did not send out a distress signal during the attack. *LIFE* magazine photographer David E. Scherman photographed the attack. *SFCB-TIM*

The famous "wanted dead or alive" photograph shot from a lifeboat by *LIFE* magazine photographer David E. Scherman just after dawn. It was kept from the Germans and later used by the Royal Navy to identify and sink the *Atlantis*. It was one of the most popular photographs ever taken before the United States entered into World War II. *TIM*

tion experts motored across to the ship to sink it. Unluckily for the Germans, *LIFE* magazine photographer David E. Scherman took pictures as quickly as possible for what he knew would be a best-selling series of photos.

After all of the crew and passengers of the *Zam Zam* were aboard the *Atlantis*, muffled roars from the erupting demolition charges were heard, and the ship slipped beneath the calm waters. One huge water-bubble explosion marked her ending, as the boilers exploded when they were engulfed in cool water. This was a common sight to the crew of the *Atlantis*, but rare to the travelers aboard the *Zam Zam*.

Captain Rogge consulted with Berlin as to what the next move was, as he now had several neutrals on his hands. Although there might be some joy in British circles that Americans were caught up in the war, Nazi Germany wanted them off the *Atlantis*. The next morning, all were surprised to see the supply ship M/V *Dresden* alongside the *Atlantis*. The *Dresden* was to take the newly acquired passengers off the raider so that it could go about its business. By noon on April 18, 1941, all of the *Zam Zam*'s passengers, crew, and their baggage were transferred to the *Dresden*. The *Atlantis* quietly sailed over the horizon, and no one knew that photographer Scherman had stashed four rolls of undeveloped film in a cleaned-out metal toothpaste container, a tube of shaving cream, and in two boxes of surgical gauze. The film was of the lifeboats and the raider from sea level that escaped confiscation by the German crew. A missionary doctor carried the contraband in his bag until they reached neutral Portugal. The German sailors did not seem to have any problems with interior pictures taken, but they wanted no shots of the exterior that might be used to identify the ship. Scherman was able to get a perfect shot that became more or less a wanted poster for the *Raider C*.

The crew of the *Dresden* built a makeshift dining room and sleeping quarters for their guests. On May 21, 1941, she tied up in Nazi-occupied France at Saint-Jean-Luz after a brief interlude while she extricated herself from an unanticipated grounding. After a heated argument between diplomatic officials, American citizens were allowed to make their way to Lisbon, Portugal, and then board another neutral ship, the SS *Serpa Pinto*. The ambulance drivers had a little longer wait and made

People leave the SS *Zam Zam* to board lifeboats in the water. Fortunately, the water was warm and calm, and there were no major casualties. It is surprising that the old liner did not sink quickly after its hull was hit by so many high-caliber shells. *SFCB–TIM*

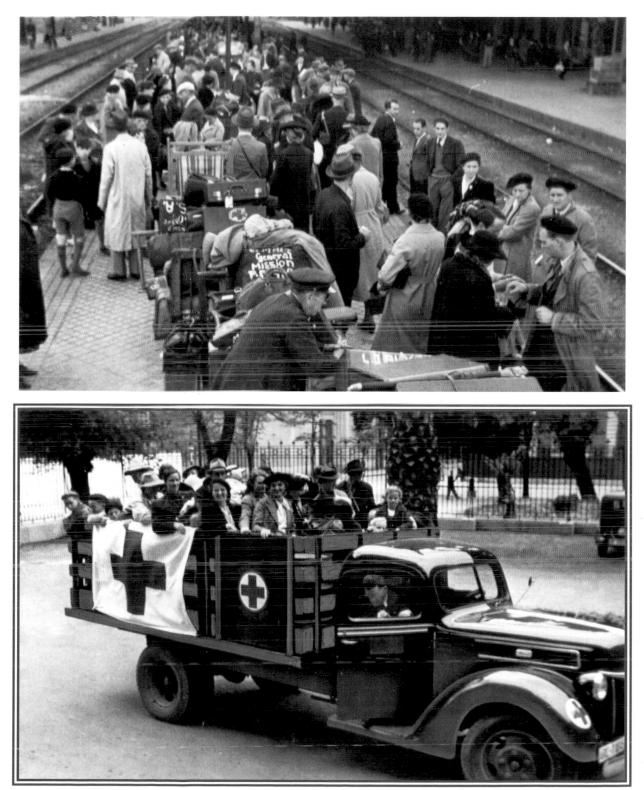

The odyssey of the SS *Zam Zam* and the passengers held by German authorities aboard the *Dresden* and in occupied France draws to a close in this photograph. Finally, in late June 1941, the neutral passengers were allowed to travel to Spain then to Lisbon, Portugal, and finally to the United States when the ordeal was over. Here, passengers wait for Red Cross trucks to carry them across the border. *SFCB–TIM*

Children of missionaries arrive in New York aboard the SS *Serpa Pinto* on June 23, 1941. *SFCB–TIM*

their way home via the USS *West Point*, a U.S. Navy transport. The other foreign nationals were interned for the duration of the war in Nazi-occupied France.

The *Zam Zam* had its revenge in the end. The photo of the *Atlantis* taken by photographer Scherman soon appeared in *LIFE* magazine and in the wardroom of every warship in the Royal Navy. The heavy cruiser HMS *Devonshire*, armed with eight 8-inch guns, located the well-disguised raider on November 22, 1941. The *Devonshire*'s scout aircraft verified that it was indeed the *Atlantis*, despite the suspicious ship's pleas that she was the SS *Polyphemus*, a Dutch freighter. The *Devonshire*'s 8-inch guns made short work of the *Atlantis*. The *Devonshire* feared a submarine attack if she stopped to verify, so the ship wisely left the area. It was a smart move by Captain Oliver of the cruiser *Devonshire*, because the U–126 was close by waiting to torpedo the cruiser if the opportunity presented itself. The U-boat towed boatloads of survivors from the *Atlantis* to safety, which was a great risk, because the submarine could not submerge during a rescue effort.

CSS H.L. Hunley *and* USS Housatonic *(1864)*

Recently appointed submariners sweated in quiet solitude in a cigar-shaped boat several feet beneath the water and prayed they would survive. The air was foul, and they were chilled, frightened, and cold. The crew was young and expected to endure hardship and even death. Their primary focus was the mission, survival, and ultimate escape from their craft. The date was February 17, 1864, just outside Charleston Harbor in South Carolina. Nine men hand-cranked the 39-foot long, 7.5-ton CSS *H.L. Hunley* and shot a 135-pound explosive into the side of the U.S. Navy blockading ship USS *Housatonic*. The men in the experimental submarine were Confederate State of America naval volunteers. Thirteen former crew men died when the CSS *H.L. Hunley* sunk during a test. After the deaths, the jet-black, iron-hulled, hand-crank-powered Confederate Navy submersible was called the "murder ship." The *Housatonic* was a thorn in the side of all of the citizens of Charleston because the federal vessel seemed to intercept every blockade runner that brought vital supplies to a starving rebel nation. To add insult to injury, it flaunted its power by periodically shelling the helpless city. The *Housatonic* had to be destroyed, and shortly after 9:00 P.M. on February 17, the 135-pound charge detonated, and the *Housatonic* sank in minutes and took five men to their death. The desperately tired, aching crew of the *H.L. Hunley* had one brief moment of intense satisfaction before its craft sank without survivors. The first successful attack by a submarine ended in tragedy and death for the entire crew, and for 136 years the iron coffin lay in silt and mud.

On August 8, 2000, after a massive and very expensive recovery effort led by author Clive Cussler, the barnacle- and mud-encrusted, 39-foot long submersible broke the water's surface near Charleston Harbor. The ecstatic cheers of thousands of onlookers greeted the almost unrecognizable shape. Aside from the *H.L. Hunley*'s recovery, many were anxious to discover what lie inside the hull. Noted maritime archeologists and naval historians speculated with some degree of hope that there would be nine mummified bodies preserved in the boat, and examining them and the artifacts aboard the *H.L. Hunley* would provide much valuable information for future generations to study. No bodies were found, but they did locate some personal items of the crew.

OSCAR-Class SSGN Kursk (2000)

A world away, on the day of jubilation in Charleston, the Russian nuclear-powered guided-missile submarine SSGN *Kursk* had been at sea for several days. It was part of a multi-ship, war-game exercise in the freezing and always hostile Barents Sea. The *Kursk*, named after a city in Russia, was one of 11 508-foot-long, 19,400-ton, full-displacement guided missile submarine cruisers. To put this into perspective, the *Kursk* was more than one-and-a-half football fields long. The *Kursk* and many of its 10 sisters had been built since the final years of the cold war. The final unit, the SSGN *Tomsk*, entered service on February 28, 1997. They are code-named OSCAR II by NATO and carry a crew of 107 men composed of 52 officers and 55 enlisted men. Many of the enlisted men are conscripts (enforced enlistment) with only six months of basic submarine training and depend on a small cadre of experienced officers to learn the difference between a periscope and the galley. When the *Kursk*, the pride of the Northern Fleet's submarine force, sailed from the Vidyayevo Naval Base near Murmansk, Russia, its complement included 11 additional personnel, for a total of 118 crew members.

The OSCAR II class is designed to remain at sea for a period of four months. To relieve the tedium of undersea life, the *Kursk* was equipped with a library, solarium, gymnasium, swimming pool, sauna, a daily glass of wine or other spirits, and facilities for pets such as dogs and cats. This class was designed for long patrols, and the vessels are able to dive 600 meters to avoid the prying ears of American submarines and surveillance ships. They were planned to be killers of large surface ships or coastal cities.

The *Kursk* was powered by two nuclear reactors that generated 98,000 horsepower. This enabled these clumsy-looking submarines to steam at 15 knots on the surface and 31 knots underwater. In a 24-hour day, the *Kursk* could put over 800 nautical miles beneath her keel.

The OSCAR IIs are armed with 28 SSN-16 stallion anti-submarine missiles that can be launched from their torpedo tubes, as well as nuclear-tipped torpedoes. The real punch of the class is in the 24 P-7 Granit SSN-19 Shipwreck guided missiles that are fired from hatches on either side of their 60-foot-wide hulls. The missiles have a 300-nautical-mile range and can be tipped with either high explosives or 300 kiloton nuclear weapons. The OSCAR IIs are primarily battle-group killers and are designed to loiter in areas where American nuclear aircraft carrier or amphibious groups are known to dwell. Their mission is simple: in the event of war, launch externally guided missiles and hope that one or more detonate near their intended targets of ship concentrations or industrialized coastal cities. If they are successful, they can destroy up to 10 percent of the U.S. Navy's force at sea in one attack or cities as large as Boston or San Francisco. If the submarines are victorious they can escape back to their home port.

On the morning of August 12, 2000, the *Kursk* launched a Chelomey Granit missile (NATO code name SSN-19 Shipwreck) that successfully hit a target hulk with a 1,600-pound warhead at a range of 200 miles.

Fortune did not continue to smile on the *Kursk* that day, however. The next evolution was the simulated firing of an SSN-16A Stallion anti-submarine rocket-boosted torpedo that is designed to kill nuclear attack and ballistic missile submarines. The Stallion fired was armed with a mini-charge of 220 pounds. Apparently, a component of the weapon ignited and caused a further explosion that damaged the boat beyond redemption.

In a statement released two years after the incident, Russian authorities admitted that the loss

HMS DEVONSHIRE (LONDON)

The HMS *Devonshire*, an older *County*-class cruiser, located and sank the *Atlantis* on November 22, 1941, in the South Atlantic. The cruiser's scout pilot and the lookouts referred to the photograph taken by *LIFE* magazine photographer Scherman. This, coupled with suspicious behavior and evasive responses to secret signals, caused the captain of the 12-year-old cruiser to open fire with his main armament as well as with his secondary 4-inch battery. The *Atlantis* attempted to respond, but it was literally blown out of the water. The SS *Zam Zam* and 21 other vessels had their revenge, and the chapters on the *Zam Zam* and the *Atlantis* were closed. The *Devonshire* survived the war and was broken up for scrap in 1954. *Author's collection*

of the ship was the direct result of an explosive charge detonating in torpedo tube number four at 11:28:26 Moscow time, which in turn ignited other torpedo charges and sent the boat to the bottom of the Barents Sea. The boat was at a depth of 66 feet when this occurred, and its periscope was raised. The submarine lost stability and began a rapid descent to the bottom. When the disabled submarine struck the seabed, the forward part of the submarine was crushed into a shapeless form.

The explosions were overheard by a U.S. Navy surveillance craft, the USNS *Loyal*, which was shadowing the exercise from a distance, and was also heard by three other submarines: the USS *Memphis* (SSN-691), an older *Los Angeles*–class attack submarine; the USS *Tennessee* (SSBN-734), an *Ohio-*

class ballistic missile submarine, and the British submarine HMS *Splendid* (S-106), an older nuclear attack boat.

The battered Russian OSCAR II crashed to a depth of 354 feet under the Barents Sea and came to rest downward at an angle of 20-plus degrees to starboard. Its escape hatch forward and escape pod in the conning tower were both rendered inoperable, and most of the crew members were already dead when the stern of the boat came to rest on the seabed.

The Russians, always cautious, did not allow any American divers to search the *Kursk* to determine if life still existed. On August 21, Norwegian divers opened the aft outer escape hatch of the *Kursk* and made other tests to determine if there was life aboard the submarine. All of the crew had been

killed. The swift flooding of all 10 watertight compartments in the hull doomed the crew. Donning survival gear and utilizing the escape hatches was apparently not possible due to the all-encompassing nature of the disaster. Divers then entered the submarine to remove the dead and commence salvage operations.

Despite the Russian government's denial, *Kursk* likely carried a full complement of defensive and offensive weapons. Submarines and surface warships rarely participate in war games or multi-ship exercises without armament. The *Kursk* was part of a small task force of Russian warships that acted out various naval scenarios in the Barents Sea. This relatively new submarine and other nuclear vessels in the Russian navy work together to appear to be a first-class blue-water fighting force. Reality indicates, however, that Russian naval capability is second-rate. Since the end

of the Cold War a decade ago, the ex–Soviet Union has literally imploded socially, spiritually, and economically, which has affected its armed forces. Inadequate and unregulated maintenance, sporadic training, and poor leadership have led the Russian navy down a path of ruin. Graft and corruption have become a way of life, and military hardware is sold out in the open. Many of its leaders and senior officers cannot accept what has happened and continue to make an effort to show the world that the Russian navy is "relevant."

Aside from being deceived by their government into false hope, Russian political and naval authorities at first refused the assistance of U.S., British, and Norwegian experts who might have been able to tell the world the truth rather than let the lie drag on for over a week. In the first days of the tragedy, the Russian naval attaché in Washington, D.C., was

The OSCAR II SSGN *Kursk* (K-141) plows through a calm sea toward the photographer. The circular hatch near the back of the boat on the upper hull is one of two escape hatches, and it is most likely the one that was undamaged on the *Kursk*.

literally taken aback by the disaster and stated that, "Moscow had issued no more information than he learned from mass media sources." His counterpart in the Ukrainian Embassy was more candid. Lt. Commander Nechyporenko had at one time been a submariner in the Soviet Northern Fleet. He stated that, "The situation was grim, and although the Russian navy possessed submarine rescue vessels, they had been either scrapped or were in poor condition." As early as three days after the incident, he offered little hope for the survival of the 118 men.

Recovery of the Dead and of the SSGN Kursk

A week after the accident, it was obvious that there was no life aboard the stricken submarine. The weather worsened, and the recovery of the crew and the aft part of the submarine was delayed. Twenty-three crew men survived for eight hours in the aft part of the boat. They succumbed to carbon monoxide poisoning from the internal fires, but some were able to leave notes and letters for loved ones.

The submersibles *MIR 1* and *MIR 2*, serviced by the M/V *Akademik Mstislav Keldysh*, a scientific research vessel, made 10 dives and confirmed that there was no foreign collision by another vessel or submarine. It was clear the loss of the *Kursk* was based on an internal problem. By August 20, 2000, it was confirmed there were no survivors.

Over the next several weeks and months, several seamen were retrieved and identified. Over a year later, agreements had been made to lift the *Kursk* off the Barents seabed and transport the damaged submarine to the Port of Roslyakovo, near the Port of Murmansk, Russia.

On September 27, 2001, the *Giant 4 Barge*, part of an international consortium including the Dutch company Mommoet-Smith, was ready to raise the *Kursk*. The basic plan was to lift the submarine with pontoons and sail slowly to a Russian port. On

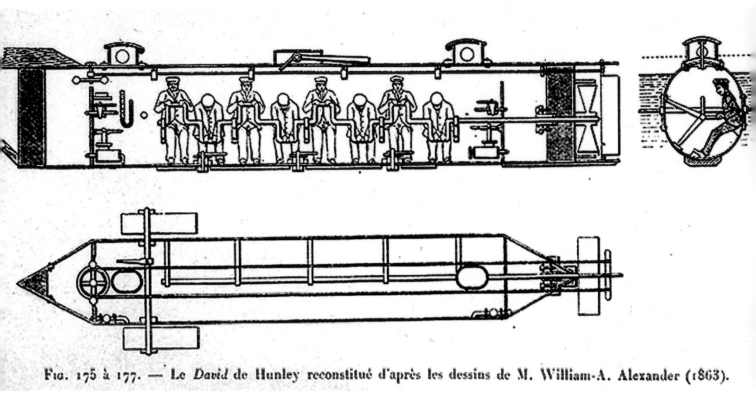

Fig. 175 à 177. — Le *David* de Hunley reconstitué d'après les dessins de M. William-A. Alexander (1863).

This is a drawing of the Confederate States Navy CSS *H.L. Hunley,* a hand-crank-powered submarine with a spar torpedo attached to its bow. Its purpose was to drive the spar into the blockading Union vessel, the USS *Housatonic* off the coast of Charleston, South Carolina. The *Housatonic* was a household word and a horrible nuisance to the local residents because it routinely shelled the city. On February 17, 1864, the torpedo worked, but both vessels were lost. The Hunley was located on August 8, 2000, by writer and adventurer Clive Cussler after an exhaustive search. *U.S. Navy*

October 23, 2001, the conning tower with the Russian state emblem met the surface of the water again after over 14 months below the surface of the Barents Sea. Russian technical specialists will thoroughly examine the boat and determine its fate.

Soviet Nuclear Submarine Accidents, Disasters, and the "Hiroshima Boat"

The West knows little about the extent of failures and accidents in various Soviet and Russian nuclear submarine shipyards and ports. What has been discovered through espionage; private organizations such as Greenpeace International; Bellona, the Norwegian watchdog agency; and Russian whistle-blowing naval officers is frightening and reminiscent of the Chernobyl nuclear accident. Including the *Kursk,* there are five known Soviet/Russian nuclear submarines that have sunk and are lying on bottom of the oceans.

It began on July 4, 1961, when the *November*-class attack submarine *K-19* had a severe nuclear reactor problem that ultimately contaminated the boat and its crew with lethal doses of radiation. Ten men died

within days, and the rest of the crew was permanently affected. Eight years later the, *K-19* collided with the American nuclear submarine USS *Gato* (SSN-615). The damage and number of deaths is unknown. From that point, the *K-19* was dubbed the "Hiroshima Boat," and Soviet submariners avoided it like the Black Death.

In the years leading up to the dissolution of the Soviet Union, seven *November*-class boats were seriously damaged with substantial loss of life. The disasters, primarily fires, that struck this class paled when compared to 13 *Hotel*-class ballistic missile submarines that were involved in one tragedy after another, most related to their nuclear powerplants.

Considering fires, collisions with shadowing U.S. Navy surface ships and submarines, and sinkings, the Soviet/Russian navy has experienced 40 known serious incidents. Five of their boats have sunk, and the loss of life is conservatively estimated at 625 souls. The sinkings began with the *November*-class attack submarine *K-8,* which suffered a fire on April 10, 1970. It sank the following day after 52 of its crew had died.

OSCAR II SSGN KURSK
(K-141)

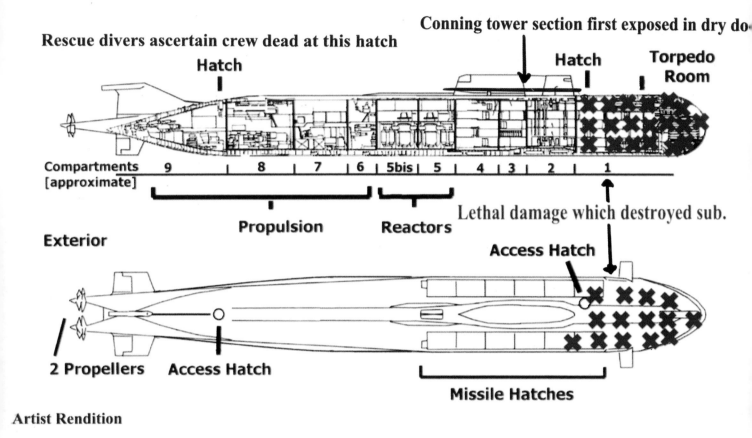

Conning tower section first exposed in dry do[ck]

Rescue divers ascertain crew dead at this hatch

Hatch

Hatch

Torpedo Room

Compartments [approximate]

9 | 8 | 7 | 6 | 5bis | 5 | 4 | 3 | 2 | 1

Propulsion

Reactors

Lethal damage which destroyed sub.

Exterior

Access Hatch

2 Propellers   **Access Hatch**

Missile Hatches

Artist Rendition

A line drawing of OSCAR II *Kursk* (K-141) that indicated the probable areas of damage from the explosion. The blast caused the vessel to immediately flood and the submarine crashed to the bottom of the sea. The aft hatch was later broke open by rescue divers, and water was the only thing to bubble out. This confirmed the entire crew had perished soon after the damage occured. *Carolyn Bonner/Federation of American Scientists*

On May 23, 1964, the *K-27* was engaged in sea trials when its reactor failed and radiation gases permeated the boat. The reactor coolant system failed, and the submarine was so badly damaged that it was abandoned and later scuttled in the Kara Sea in 1981.

A *Yankee*-class *K-219* had an explosion in one of its ballistic missile tubes north of Bermuda in the Atlantic in early October 1986. Despite efforts to control the damage, the boat sank on October 6, 1986, and took four crew members and 16 SSN-6 Serb nuclear-tipped ICBMs with it.

One of the most prominent losses was the *K-278 Mike*-class *Komsomolets*. It was a new type of boat sheathed in a titanium hull and could dive more than

3,000 feet, which is beyond the reach of any contemporary anti-submarine weapon in the West. On April 7, 1989, the *Komsomolets* was ravaged by fire in the Norwegian Sea on its way back to base. The submarine finally sank with its 41 crew members. A Soviet rescue ship took on 25 survivors and 5 dead. There was inadequate escape equipment and too few rafts. Most of these had drifted too far from the sinking boat.

There have been a number of collisions between U.S. warships and Soviet submarines aside from the *K-19* and the *Gato* (SSN-615). An *Echo II K-557* collided with the USS *Tautog* (SSN-639) on June 20, 1970, in the Pacific. The *Echo II* was a cruise missile attack submarine, and it barely made it back to base. On June 14, 1973, another *Echo II*, the *K-56,* collided with the Soviet ship M/V *Akademik Berg* in Soviet waters and killed 27 crew members. In 1977, an *Echo I* nuclear attack boat struck the escort USS *Voge* (FF-1047) in the Mediterranean, and both ships suffered extensive damage. In 1983, a *Victor III* became entangled in the towed array of the ASW frigate USS *McCloy* (FF-1038), just off the South Carolina coast. The Soviet attack submarine was towed to Cuba for repairs. A year later, on March 21, 1984, a *Victor I* attack boat collided with the USS *Kitty Hawk* (CV 63) in the Sea of Japan. The extent of damage was unknown.

Most of their difficulties have resulted from reactor coolant leakage, fire, and premature explosions. The U.S. Navy has had its share of similar tragedies with the loss of the nuclear attack submarine USS *Thresher* and 129 lives in 1963 and the USS *Scorpion* and 99 lives in 1968. There is strong evidence that the *Scorpion* was traveling at or near periscope depth when a faulty trash ejector allowed water to enter and flood the battery bank. This caused fire, explosion, and a loss of control—circumstances somewhat similar to the *Kursk*. The *Scorpion* imploded and was shattered beyond recognition as it hit the bottom of the Atlantic 10,000 feet down.

The life of a submariner in any navy is fraught with danger, and accidents can and do happen. In-depth training, good supervision, high recruitment standards, and well-maintained equipment lower the risk of failure appreciably, but this is sometimes not enough. A rescue can happen only under optimum conditions. Western submariners have a better chance of survival in the event of a crisis, but, unfortunately, this is not so in the Russian navy. Their leadership has again painfully learned that sending a crew of conscripts on a poorly maintained vessel into harm's way is sometimes a one-way voyage.

CHAPTER 6

The *Oregon Responder* is moored at Astoria, Oregon, and is one of many craft ready to attack an oil spill on the West Coast. Similar craft can be found in Everett, Washington; San Francisco; and other major ports. A crew stands by and is ready to go at a moment's notice. *Author's collection*

IMPROVING SAFETY AT SEA FOR MARINERS, PORTS, AND VESSELS

Once an individual chooses a life of the sea or a related profession, there are no real guarantees of safety. Western nations have progressed the most in promoting security due to a number of reasons, including the value of life, replacements costs of shipping and port facilities, and the interruption or destruction of trade. A simple example rests with interrupting the flow of crude oil from the North Slope, North Sea, or Middle East. Until the world comes up with a better method of powering itself and its machinery, oil is our most valuable commodity as an energy resource. Wars are fought over it, and even a small interference in the flow of black gold will have long-lasting effects on nations. Japan rose as a military power based on imported raw resources and oil from Indonesia. Without the oil, the nation would have starved within 18 months.

Unfortunately, nations that are dependent on the sea, but too poor to afford decent protection for their mariners, allow ships to go to sea that are all but sinking from rust spots, leak oil, and have ineffective lifesaving equipment. In these cases, mariners take their chances by going to sea. One group that has become extremely outspoken is the United Filipino Seafarers in the Philippine Islands. Each day, their members put condemned ships and worn-out, overcrowded ferry boats to sea. If something does happen, there is no hope of being saved because the Philippine Coast Guard is incapable of saving lives. Some of its most modern vessels are leftover ships from World War II or Vietnam. These vessels do not have the electronic equipment nor speed to get to a major disaster and save lives, let alone the resources to enforce laws against huge multinational shipping conglomerates that do not maintain or install sufficient safety equipment on their passenger and cargo vessels.

Comparatively, the United States and other Western nations periodically build and deploy new vessels and aircraft to save lives at sea and carry out inspection services. Various major ports participate in oil spill recovery operations, and specialized vessels are stationed along the coasts of the United States for that purpose.

Most, if not all, harbors have fire boats that are supplemented by U.S. Coast Guard vessels with firefighting capability. The idea of another Texas City Disaster is too horrible to imagine. It took time to collect data from studies, redesign the ports, build modern firefighting boats, and change the mindset from lax to very cautious.

Today, the United States and many other nations have maritime institutions that train engineers and deck officers. They are thoroughly trained in safety protocol, and one of the first issues is how to survive in the water. Among others, there are maritime schools in California, Massachusetts, New York, as well as the Merchant Marine Academy in Kings Point, New York. Students are taught the most up-to-date methods in safe shipping, and the accident rate has dropped. This, along with the U.S. Coast Guard, has added a new dimension to safe shipping in American ports.

The U.S. Coast Guard and Coast Guard Auxiliary

The U.S. Coast Guard is known as America's maritime guardian, and it has responded to maritime troubles since its formation in 1790. The Coast Guard now is responsible for maritime security, maritime safety, protection of natural resources, maritime mobility, and national defense in times of war.

The *Guardian*, a San Francisco Fire Department fire boat, is moored under the Bay Bridge in August 2002. The *Guardian* is 50 years old and can pump 24,000 gallons per minute. The boat goes into dry dock every two to three years for an overhaul, and everything is kept in order for when the boat is called to duty. *Author's collection*

One of the major programs the U.S. Coast Guard has become engaged in is Port State Control. The basic idea is to prevent substandard vessels from entering and remaining in U.S. ports just because they fly a flag of convenience. As it stands, 95 percent of all passenger ships are foreign flagged, and 75 percent of all cargo ships also fly the flag of another nation. Oil rigs and ships that fly the American flag are also inspected. The U.S. Coast Guard does what is necessary to bring ships and other maritime operations in concert with U.S. safety rules and regulations.

The U.S. Coast Guard performs search and rescue (SAR) missions as far out at sea as possible. They operate C-130 Hercules, or "thundering pigs," that can travel far out to sea to provide rafts and survival equipment. For inshore work, the HH-60 Jayhawk helicopter rescues crews from vessels that have run aground or are in danger. In 2002, the U.S. Coast Guard saved 3,680 lives and prevented 117,780 pounds of processed cocaine from crossing U.S. borders.

For seagoing SAR or drug-interdiction patrols, the U.S. Coast Guard has a mixture of high- and medium-endurance cutters. There are a number of other craft that perform harbor patrol, tend buoys, and keep ports free of ice in the Great Lakes and in Alaska. The Coast Guard can turn a dime into a quarter, and it knows how use its resources to best affect. Much of its equipment, aircraft, and boats are

Cadets at the California Maritime Academy perform a drill aboard the school ship, the TS *Golden Bear. Author's collection*

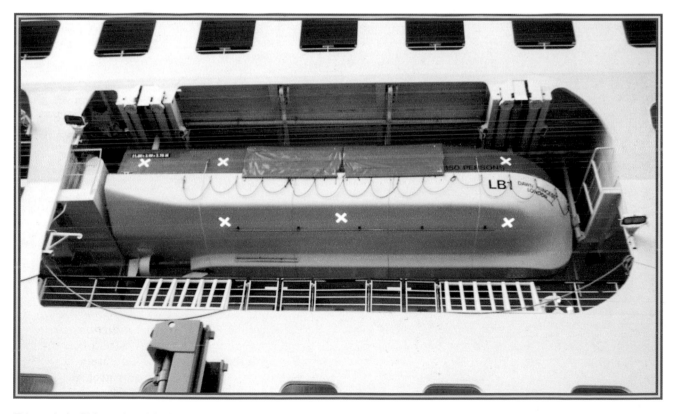

This particular lifeboat aboard the M/V *Dawn Princess* is recessed for easy boarding for passengers. After the passengers are seated, the boat slides out and is lowered to the water. *Courtesy Cleo Yancy*

A current high-endurance cutter, the U.S. Coast Guard cutter *Hamilton* (WHEC 715), is based out of San Diego, California. These vessels are quite old and have been updated since the Vietnam War. Under the U.S. Coast Guard Deepwater Program, the *Hamilton* will ultimately be replaced by the 410-foot National Security Cutter. *Author's collection*

The coastal buoy-tender *George Cobb* (WLM-564) in the summer of 2002. The *George Cobb* is a 175-foot *Keeper*-class buoy-tender that was built in Marinette, Wisconsin, and was recently added to the fleet of newer vessels in the U.S. Coast Guard. The *George Cobb* is capable of 12 knots and displaces 840 tons fully loaded. *Author's collection by Melissa Lanzaro*

out of date, and the U.S. Coast Guard needs a large infusion of taxpayer dollars to improve its ability to meet its commitments and be a cornerstone of the Department of Homeland Security. This translates to the much-discussed and now-planned Integrated Deepwater System.

The U.S. Coast Guard and the Integrated Deepwater System

In essence, the Integrated Deepwater System is a fully integrated and modernized upgrade of the U.S. Coast Guard that uses a systems approach to its functions and missions. For years, the U.S. Coast Guard, which is an integral part of homeland defense, has had to make do with whatever it could squeeze out of the government or other agencies just to operate. Despite the obvious need for a coast guard and the desperate need this nation has for a maritime guardian, funds have not been as forthcoming as they have for other major Department of Defense operations.

This popular 47-foot aluminum search and rescue craft can roll over and resume operations. These craft can go anywhere there is rough water. The crews are trained at the mouth of the Columbia River, also know as the Pacific Graveyard of ships. The crews go out when the instructor is certain the swell and waves will roll the craft over and over. *Author's collection*

The *Sockeye* is a *Marine Protector*-class enforcement and search and rescue craft based out of Bodega Bay, California. It is part of what will be the Deepwater System. The Deepwater System will evolve over a period of years, and some areas are already underway. The *Sockeye* is an 87-foot-long vessel armed with two 50-caliber machine guns. It was placed in service in January 2002 at Bodega Bay, California. *Author's collection*

The Yerba Buena Island Coast Guard Base is where the craft that guard the San Francisco Bay area are moored. The craft in the center of the frame, the *Point Brower* (WPB-82372), dates back to the Vietnam War and is one of two left over from that conflict. The *Point*-class cutter, with guns manned, watched over the August ceremonies when the USS *McCampbell* (DDG-85, *Aegis*-class destroyer) was commissioned in San Francisco. *Author's collection*

The Integrated Deepwater System will upgrade certain modern units, discard older systems, and add items such as HAE-UAV unmanned air vehicles for surveillance of up to 38 hours and a range of 12,500 nautical miles. This unmanned air vehicle can send real-time images back to a cutter or shore station and save crew time. Improved helicopters (AB-139 VRS) that can be carried by almost all helicopter-capable cutters and surface ship improvements will include the National Security Cutter (NSC), which is 421 feet in length and carries helicopters and unmanned

vehicles with an endurance of 60 days and a range of 12,000 miles. The crew requirement is 82 personnel that are highly trained electronics technicians. Maritime patrol aircraft will replace the aging fleet of C-130 Hercules with a range of 3,055 nautical miles and are fully integrated with all other surface ship and unmanned flight assets.

In other words, the U.S. Coast Guard will rely on electronics to make up for its lack of staff, but in the end, a rescue swimmer will jump out of the improved helicopter to pull a terrified person to safety.

BIBLIOGRAPHY

I. PRIMARY MATERIALS/Manuscripts and Photo Files

20th Century Fox/Paramount Pictures
Bonner, Kermit H., Jr.
Bonner, Kermit H., Sr.
Burgess, Richard. U.S. Navy League
Call Bulletin Newspaper Files 1994;
    Treasure Island Museum
Carnival Cruise Lines – Public Affairs Office
Cavas, Chris; *Navy Times*
Cunard Line
Evonuk, Lt. (JG) Pete; U.S. Coast Guard
    Sacramento (Search and Rescue)
Hughes, CPO Sean; Pearl Harbor U.S. Navy
James Cameron; Director, *Titanic*
Lane, PO; U.S. Coast Guard, Alameda, California
Lightstorm Entertainment
Navy League of the United States – *Seven Seas*
Portland, Oregon, PAO
Princess Cruises
Ramer, LCDR Kevin; U.S. Coast Guard, Yerba
    Buena Island
Ramirez, Nelson R.; President, United
    Filipino Seafarers
Reed, Terry; Part-time manager Naval Station
Reeves, CPO Darren; U.S. Coast Guard
Royal Caribbean Cruise Lines
Sea Classics – Challenge Publications
    Ed Schnepf, Editor
Sellers, Comdr. Karen; U.S. Coast Guard
Treasure Island Museum Photo Files
U.S. Coast Guard; Publication 1 and Deepwater Project
U.S. Navy Internet Site; www.navy.mil
Yancy, Cleo

II. SECONDARY MATERIALS
A. Books, Monographs, Treaties

Ambrose, A. J. (Editor). *Jane's Merchant Review*.
    Jane's: 1982.
Bonner, Kit, and Carolyn Bonner. *Warship Boneyards*. MBI
Publishing Company: 2000.
Bonnett, Wayne. *Build Ships*. Wingate Press: 1999.
Bonsall, Thomas E. *Titanic*. Gallery Books: 1987.

Dunn, Laurence. *Liners and Their Recognition*.
    The Blackmore Press: 1954.
Gibbs, Jim. *Peril at Sea*. Schiffer Publishing: 1986.
Hudson, Kenneth and Ann Nicholls. *Tragedy on the
    High Seas*. A & W Publishers: 1979
Maddocks, Melvin. *The Great Liners*. Time-Life
    Books: 1978.
McMillan, Beverly, and Stanley Lehrer. *Titanic
    –Fortune and Fate*. Simon & Schuster: 1998.
Miller, William H., Jr. *Great Cruise Ships and Ocean
    Liners From 1954 to 1986: A Photographic Survey*.
    Dover Publications: 1988.
Morris, Douglas. *Cruisers of the Royal and
    Commonwealth Navies Since 1879*.
    Maritime Books: 1987.
Perkes, Dan. *Eyewitness to Disaster*. Hammond
    Incorporated: 1976 and Gallery Books: 1985.
Pitt, Barrie. *The Battle of the Atlantic*. Time Life
    Books: 1977.
Quinn, William P. *Shipwrecks Along the Atlantic Coast*.
    Parnassus Imprints: 1988.
Robertson, Morgan. *The Wreck of the Titan Or Futility*.
    M F Mansfield:1898 and Buccaneer Books: 1991.
Silverstone, Paul H. *U.S. Warships of World War II*.
    Doubleday and Company: 1970, 1989.
Stephens, Hugh W. *The Texas City Disaster 1947*.
    University of Texas Press: 1947, 1997.

B. Other Sources/Materials
American Bureau of Shipping
Interviews with U.S. Coast Guard (Search and Rescue)
    personnel Interviews with leadership of United
    Filipino Seafarers Union and various government
    officials from the Philippines
Interviews with San Francisco Fireboat staff and tour
    of fireboat *Guardian*
Observations of U.S. Coast Guard (Search and
    Rescue) operations from the air
Surface Warfare; Dick Cole, Editor
Tour of cruise ship *Ecstasy* and review of new
    safety procedures
University of Balitmore-Steamship Historical
    Society, Ann House, Librarian
Various cruise and passenger liner brochures

I NDEX

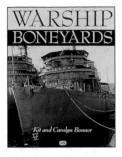
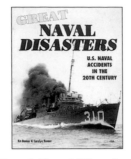

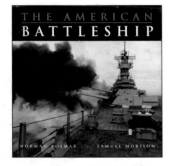

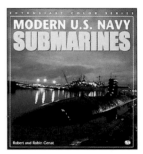

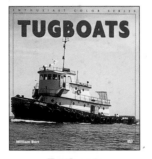